OVER-55
Conniptions
An Old Biddy Battles Aging

Gerri Almand

BROWN POSEY PRESS

an imprint of Sunbury Press, Inc.
Mechanicsburg, PA USA

BROWN POSEY PRESS

an imprint of Sunbury Press, Inc.
Mechanicsburg, PA USA

For information about special discounts for bulk purchases, please contact Sunbury Press Orders Dept. at (855) 338-8359 or orders@sunburypress.com.

To request one of our authors for speaking engagements or book signings, please contact Sunbury Press Publicity Dept. at publicity@sunburypress.com.

FIRST BROWN POSEY PRESS EDITION: December 2025

Set in Adobe Garamond | Interior design by Crystal Devine | Cover design by Lawrence Knorr | Edited by Gabrielle Kirk.

Publisher's Cataloging-in-Publication Data
Names: Almand, Gerri, author.
Title: Over-55 conniptions : an old biddy battles aging / Gerri Almand.
Description: First trade paperback edition. | Mechanicsburg, PA : Brown Posey Press, 2025.
Summary: A poignant and hysterical look at facing major life changes. Health issues drive an older couple to abandon full-time RVing and move into an over-55 community. The author rails against aging while re-discovering her own resiliency. Filled with humor, angst, and touching insights, this book will delight anyone over the age of forty.
Identifiers: ISBN : 1-979-8-88819-381-5 (softcover).
Subjects: HUMOR / Topic / Aging | FAMILY & RELATIONSHIPS / Life Stages / Later Years | SELF-HELP / Aging.

Designed in the USA
0 1 1 2 3 5 8 13 21 34 55

For the Love of Books!

Contents

Foreword

I never dreamed when my husband and I plopped ourselves down on the West Coast that I'd experience such an onslaught of intense and conflicting emotions—anger, euphoria, bewilderment, optimism, despair, and occasionally pure, unadulterated terror, to name a few. We'd been full-time RVers for almost three years when medical issues brought our nomadic lifestyle to a screeching halt. We were also coming out of the pandemic, a trauma that affected me in ways I'll never fully understand.

Over two years later, I understand my struggle to adjust to a sedentary lifestyle had not been about giving up our freedom as nomads because of our disintegrating bodies. It had been about facing my own mortality. We moved into an over-55 community, and for the first time, I saw deterioration and death heading my way. I had never thought I'd get old and die; that happened to other people. Old people.

In the beginning, I felt exhilarated at the new opportunities afforded by a fixed address on the other side of the country. I could make different choices and set up different priorities this time around. Our new over-55 community, however, made my gyroscope writhe from the inside out, convoluting and twisting into bewildering knots and tangles. I alternated between feeling excited at being able to redefine myself to feeling wretchedly untethered in an environment so eerie and unfamiliar I feared I'd never find gravity again.

The characters, settings, and events described in this book are based on real people and situations. I hope any friends and neighbors who read these words and believe they see themselves in the anecdotes will forgive me if they feel misrepresented. I dug my way through tons of emotional, social, and cultural flotsam to adjust and realign my perspectives. My issues had nothing to do with anyone I know or have written about. They were always, 100 percent, about me. I have railed, not about my friends or neighbors but about watching myself and my husband grow older, complete with all our new medical diagnoses, deteriorating body parts, and pathetic struggles to rebuild our lives in what still sometimes feels like a foreign land.

If I can ease feelings of pain, fear, or sadness about growing old in a single reader, and if I can bring a nod of understanding or a few chuckles along the way, then this book will have satisfied my reasons for writing it.

Getting old is inevitable. I hope my readers will handle it with more grace than I have managed so far. But rest assured, I am trying.

Acknowledgments

Many thanks to the folks who have read multiple chapters of this tirade-turned-acceptance. You helped me find my voice, pointed out myriad ways to strengthen my writing skills, and helped me learn a bit more tolerance and patience, both of myself and of others. These excellent writers and authors are Charlie Cousins, David Fryer, Lex LeFay, Susan Parman, and Jill Amy Sager, all members of the Willamette Writers in Oregon. Your technical, storytelling skills are excellent, your creativity inspired and awed, and your voices still resonate in my head every time I sit down to write.

To my beta readers, Tom Rhiel, Aleida Socarras, Jill Amy Sager, Jim Beane, Michael Foster, and Pat Anderson, your time, energy, and feedback helped shape the manuscript into its current iteration. Thank you. Your friendships mean so much to me.

To my over-55 neighbors, you are wonderful role models of hope, strength, and perseverance. You have helped me grow and adjust to my new life in Oregon.

To my husband Michael Hamlin, I appreciate your patience and support more than I can express. I know you'd rather I not spend so much time gardening and sitting at my laptop. I promise to do better from now on.

CHAPTER 1

We Need to Talk

January 2022

"You would have loved it," my excited husband almost shouted as he entered our motorhome toting a big basket of clean but unfolded clothes. "There's this grizzled old man in the laundry room, shirttail untucked and at least a three-day stubble of whiskers on his face, and he just blurted out to no one in particular that his ex-wife ruined his life."

Michael had just returned from the RV park's laundry room. I'd ordinarily have been the one doing the laundry, but I was lying in bed with my leg elevated, feeling ridiculously sorry for myself.

"What happened then?" I eased myself off the bed so Michael could dump out the clothes. I'd fold since he'd done the washing and drying. Getting out of bed felt good. I needed to stretch and move around a bit, put an end to this pity party I was wallowing in.

"Well," Michael said, "he went on to explain that they'd planned to live here in the park year-round except for summers, but then, after a couple of years, his wife just up and announced she wanted to live in a house."

"Was anyone in the laundry room paying attention to this dude?"

"Oh, yes. There were probably eight or ten folks in there, and this guy had everyone's attention. He was loud, had a heavy Boston accent, and you could almost see venom spewing from his mouth. He went on to report that his wife took half his money, half his furniture, and half of everything he owned and then moved into a condo with her sister."

Michael took off his coat and turned the thermostat up a couple of degrees. There'd been a bit of snow the night before, and while most of it had melted, temps were still in the low forties outside. Neither of us was happy about being stuck in the dead of winter in this God-forsaken RV park in Coarsegold, California, thirty-five miles east of Fresno and twenty miles west of Yosemite National Park. At least the foothills were gorgeous to look at, with Manzanita trees, scrub pines, and huge boulders nestled in the rolling foothills of the Sierra Mountains. Creek beds twisted through the rolling rocky terrain and were slowly filling as snow melted at the higher elevations and flooded the gullies. Those creek beds had been bone-dry when we arrived in late October. A neighbor in the park had told us water levels would rise as winter progressed and possibly flood the surrounding areas by spring.

"Sorry I didn't stick around long enough to hear how the conversation ended. Some old woman started asking him questions about it, and by the time I left, it sounded like the guy was trying to pick her up. I don't think she was falling for it though."

"Seniors looking for love, huh? Guess this'd be a pretty good place for a guy to find a wife though. Women seem to outnumber the men around here at least two to one."

"You're probably right, but this poor guy needs to up his game a bit if he wants to get lucky."

"I think old men think a lot more about old women than old women think about old men," I said. "From what I've seen, most women who RV by themselves are pretty independent, probably wouldn't even want a man."

"Not sure I agree with that."

You wouldn't, I thought. You're a man.

We'd been RVing for almost seven years, and the number of women we'd met who were RVing by themselves had surprised me. I sometimes wondered what I'd do with this motorhome if something happened to

Michael. Would I keep going, or would I sell it and look for a townhouse or condo somewhere? I glanced down at my bandaged leg and realized I might be the one to go first, making any further speculation a moot point.

But Michael's eavesdropped laundry room conversation had triggered an epiphany, a jolt so profound I couldn't believe I hadn't seen it before. Just like that man's ex-wife, I suddenly knew, deep in my heart, that I, too, wanted a house.

I finished folding the laundry and started putting it away, not yet ready to share my new insight of wanting to settle down. I needed time to think about it, to figure out how to broach the subject, and to try to anticipate my husband's reaction. Although relieved to have seen a truth I suspected my subconscious had hidden from me for months, I wasn't sure how Michael would react. He loved RVing and our nomadic lifestyle. I hated to think that one day he might be a bitter disheveled old man in an RV park laundry room, hitting on old women and complaining about his ex-wife.

Yes. Michael and I needed to talk.

CHAPTER 2

I Want It All

Retiring at age sixty-two had felt luxurious. Although weary from the daily grind of a forty-year social work career, I still felt energetic and vibrant. I'd spent most of my career sitting inside offices. Now I wanted to be outside, physical rather than cerebral, and spontaneous rather than bound by daily schedules.

My younger husband Michael had continued working for another five years as I gardened with a passion in my suburban yard in Tampa, Florida. Life was good. I was exactly where I wanted and needed to be.

However, after Michael retired, his restlessness derailed me from my contented retirement bliss. Although I'd tried to convince him before retirement that he needed to find hobbies and interests, he didn't heed my sage advice. Instead, he came up with the half-baked idea that we should buy an RV and see the country.

"It'll be okay, Little Gerri." My hubby's voice oozed syrup. "We'll hire Paul to keep up the yard, and Anita can water your orchids."

"You don't understand." I controlled the speed and volume of my voice despite wanting to scream obscenities at this selfish boor I'd married. "They don't *know* my plants like I do. My plants will all die." How could he even consider asking me to leave my garden?

"RV travel will be good for you," he said. "You'll love it, I promise."

How the hell did he think he could promise me that? I'd always been a homebody, a quintessential nest builder. I'd traveled enough in my younger years to know that no matter how many countries I went to, I'd never get to them all. Also, the bragging I'd heard from many travelers about their adventures turned me off. I didn't like the preening and one-up-man-ship games people played with each other when comparing adventures. At this age, I could satisfy exotic destination fixes by reading books and watching documentaries.

Our RV negotiations, at times heated and emotional, lasted six months before I caved in. In some ways, RV travel was not even travel since folks lived in their "home" on the road. Partly, Michael just wore me down with his nonstop pressure, but the other part was that I began to share his vision. I remembered those iconic old stories from interviews with nursing home patients asking about the things they regretted most in their lives. Invariably, the regrets were over the roads not taken, the opportunities turned down. I was sixty-seven years old and Michael sixty-five when we bought our first motorhome in 2015 and took off on the road.

After several long RV trips, I'd come to realize that it was a lot of work to maintain both an RV and a house. Preparing the house for a four-to-six-month absence, arranging for yard care, convincing pharmacists to override medication refill dates, instructing the next-door neighbor as to what mail to open, scan, and email to us, and attending to myriad other details left me exhausted. While abandoning one's routine to go off into the sunset felt liberating and exhilarating, the effort needed to make it happen was huge. This was an aspect of RV travel I don't think my husband ever understood. He was the dreamer, and I was the one who took care of the endless details that resulted in smooth trips with few surprises or inconveniences.

Invariably, when we'd return home from these long road trips, most of them lasting three to six months, we'd find things that had gone wrong with the house while we'd been off galivanting. The disposal had frozen, squirrels had built a nest in the attic, or some other bizarre thing had happened that required attention. One time we returned to find a small grove of avocado trees almost four feet tall along a backyard fencerow, which I'd certainly not planted. I never figured out how they got there. Weeds overtook the flowerbeds, orchids on the lanai died from neglect, and mealy bugs invariably found their way to at least a couple of potted succulents. Sometimes I wondered if gremlins invaded our property while we were gone. By the time I'd caught up on all the plant catastrophes and house repairs, Michael would be well into planning our next long road trip.

I always felt like I did most of the work of our RV travels, but Michael argued that he did more than half. This division of labor was an ongoing point of contention. Plus, he seemed to think that sitting in front of his iPad, planning routes and destinations, was equal to my making multiple trips between the rig and the house each time we either left or returned. This included both packing and unpacking and enough steps to register in miles. The unloading of the rig after a long trip was the worst. There would be several loads of clothes and linens to wash and dry, food from the RV to process back into the kitchen, and a deep cleaning of the interior of the motorhome before we returned it to storage.

My resistance to RVing waned as I discovered the thrill of being fancy-free out in the world. I felt safe and snug like a turtle in my shell in our 26-ft. Class C motorhome. I had everything I needed or wanted within arm's reach. While I'd previously spent time keeping a home and garden, I now spent time reading, writing, bicycling, and hiking. I came to see the value of this new way of living. On the road, I learned to relax, live in the moment, and appreciate a new level of freedom. Nomadism reduced life to only the essentials and left me light and free. I realized I'd never really understood minimalism before despite having declared Henry David Thoreau my hero decades earlier.

"I can't live like this," I'd moan each time as we either packed or unpacked the RV. "It's just too much work." I admitted, though, that RV travel had given me many of the things I'd wanted in my retirement. I was outside more than inside, more physical than cerebral, and free rather than confined. I understood, too, that losing a few plants here and there was perhaps a small price to pay for the stimulation and rewards of watching dolphins play in the Pacific Ocean, seeing grizzly bear mothers and their cubs in the wilds of Alaska, or even spending six unexpected but fun weeks in Austin, Texas, when Michael broke his leg.

The initial resistance to RVing gave way to something more complex and difficult to reconcile. I found I wanted to live on the road just as much as I wanted my beautiful house, yard, and plants in Tampa. I knew it was impossible, but I wanted it all.

I've often thought of my husband as insatiable in his quest for adventure and fun. After only a couple of years of RVing, he started trying to convince me to become a full-time RVer. It took three years, but eventually he won, or maybe I finally decided on my own. In early 2020, after five years of taking two or three long road trips each year, we upgraded to a Class A motorhome, sold the house in Florida, and became vagabonds.

"We're too old to be out on the road like this," I said to Michael many times during that first year on the road. "How long do you think our health will hold out?"

"The way I see it, we need to just keep truckin' as long as we can. Maybe we can keep traveling for ten more years," Michael said, "and then we settle down when the transmission falls out of the RV."

When the transmission falls out of the RV became our running joke. Yes, that's when we'd give up this lifestyle. "Maybe it'll fall out right here," I'd said while we spent a month in Flagstaff, Arizona.

"Nope, we need to go back to Santa Fe, New Mexico. Maybe I could get the hammer and bang on the hood, see if I could loosen the thing up and make it fall," Michael said with a laugh.

"When are we going back to the East Coast?" I'd asked. "We got stuck on the West Coast when the pandemic erupted, but I really fell in love with Knoxville, Tennessee, if you'll remember. And oh, my goodness, what about Burlington, Vermont? Wasn't that a beautiful little town right on Lake Champlain?"

"There have been too many good places to even count. I'd go back to Colorado, maybe Cripple Creek or Leadville."

"Too friggin' cold," I said. "Remember when you tried to talk me into us renting a house there for the winter, a place where it gets forty degrees below freezing on a regular basis? Thank you very much, but no. While I never want to go back to the heat, humidity, and mosquitos in Florida, I don't want to live in a place that gets that cold."

At our ages, however, we knew our time on the road was finite and, in time, we'd have to settle down again. We vowed, for as long as we could, to suck all the marrow possible from the proverbial travel bones. And to my surprise, living on the road in a small motorhome soon felt as natural as living in a sticks-and-bricks house.

In time, although it proved to be a royal pain in the butt, I even figured out how to partially satisfy my longing for gardening. I bought a few hardy potted plants for the RV and moved them in and out of the motorhome every time we parked for longer than one night. I also insisted that we visit almost every botanical garden we came within fifty miles of. In time, I no longer missed the aching muscles from digging holes and hauling forty-pound bags of fertilizer, the mosquito bites and miserable heat and humidity of Florida summers, and all that dirt that used to accumulate under my fingernails, no matter what kind of gardening gloves I wore.

Life was incredibly good in those days, and I had no trouble believing that taking off fulltime in an RV was the best decision we'd ever made. Life was one exciting adventure after another, and I felt I could go on forever living as a nomad.

The pandemic affected our RV travel in more ways than we could count. Many places we'd wanted to go and things we wanted to see were no longer options because they had shut down. We were afraid to go into buildings, and the instant connections with fellow campers we used to feel in campgrounds disappeared. Everyone acted scared of everybody not in their immediate family.

Michael and I were in Texas when the pandemic erupted, where we didn't know a soul. We considered trying to return to Florida but worried about campground closures on the way back, gasoline and grocery availability on the highways, and mandatory quarantines if we were able to make it back to Florida. Given all the concerns and unknowns, we opted to wait out the pandemic in the RV.

Within a couple of months of the pandemic, I was feeling more socially isolated than I'd ever felt. On the other hand, we had tremendous freedom and flexibility sitting through a raging pandemic in a motorhome. We developed a pattern of moving every two to four weeks, always in search of pleasant weather and sparsely populated areas with low incidences of the coronavirus. We slowly made our way across the country to the West Coast.

But we were not the only ones enjoying nomadism during the pandemic. Reservations in campgrounds became harder to snag as RV sales soared. By the end of 2021, RVs were hard to find. Demand had surged because of covid restrictions, and RV manufacturers couldn't roll them off the assembly lines fast enough.

Our primary care physician back in Florida had faithfully attended to our prescription refills during 2020 and early 2021 with orders for lab work every six months. But by the middle of 2021, she refused to see us through Telehealth any longer. "Someone needs to put a stethoscope to your chest to make sure you're still alive," she said. "You must go in person to see a doctor."

"This is definitely the handwriting on the wall," I said to Michael. "We need to figure out where we can line up doctor and dentist appointments, plus we both need to see an ophthalmologist."

"We've got to be proactive," Michael said. "It's been too long since we've had any kind of medical care."

At this time, I was seventy-four and Michael was seventy-two. "We're not spring chickens anymore," I said, "and I've got a feeling doctors are going to find a couple of concerns with both of us this time around."

I had no idea how prophetic my words would become.

CHAPTER 3

The Transmission Falters

Funny how that transmission in the RV began to grumble before we even realized it was happening. We survived the first year of the pandemic in near isolation but nevertheless in high spirits. We learned the ins and outs of living as nomads and gradually built up a support system of fellow RVers. We were having the time of our lives. However, the need for medical care haunted in the background, creating the feeling that we were on a blissful, unending vacation when we knew it wasn't so.

"Guess we'd better pull out the atlas and start picking a place to schedule doctor appointments," Michael said.

"I've got my heart set on the summer on the Olympic Peninsula," I said. "Maybe we can look for a place along our route north." We were in Desert Hot Springs at the time, waiting for our Covid vaccine appointments and eager to get back on the road. The desert had been a wonderful place to spend the winter, but it was now March, and the temperature was approaching 100 degrees. Not to mention that we'd already seen two sidewinders in our RV park. I did not like rattlesnakes one bit.

We studied the routes to Sequim, Washington, where we'd been lucky to snag a three-week reservation in an RV park. Our spontaneity was a definite liability when it came to summertime camping on the Olympic Peninsula. We should have started planning months before we did.

We chose Eugene, Oregon as a good spot for medical care. A metropolitan area of about 300,000, Eugene was the home of the University of Oregon and a decent-sized middle-class community. We got on our cell phones and started exploring medical groups and specialists. Within a week or so, we'd scheduled physicals with a primary care physician, dental and eye exams, and a dermatology appointment for me. We assumed six weeks in Eugene would be more than sufficient to get our clean bills of health and be on our way north.

We arrived in Eugene in early April 2021 and started with the physical exams. We'd failed to factor in all the other tests and procedures our doctor would want, things like blood work, chest X-rays, bone density tests, mammograms, CAT scans, and more. All the add-ons took another six weeks to complete. Finally, three months after our arrival, we were on our way north but with instructions to return in six months for follow-ups.

"Whew. That was certainly a lot of work," I said. "And what's with this six-month follow-up business? In Tampa, our doctors were happy to see us once a year."

"Guess things got a bit out of control during the pandemic," Michael said. "Plus, we're a couple of years older now. This was bound to happen eventually."

Six months later during a follow-up appointment with the dermatologist in Eugene on our way back south for the winter, the transmission began to wobble. "I'm doing a biopsy of this lesion on your leg," my doctor said, "and I can tell you already you're going to need Mohs surgery. We'd better get this scheduled as soon as possible."

"But we're on our way to California for the winter," I told her. It was October. The rainy season in the Pacific Northwest had started, and temperatures were already dipping into the forties at night. Our plan was to return to the RV park in Desert Hot Springs where we'd hunkered down for over four months during the Covid winter of 2020-21 with our RV club.

"You can it get scheduled wherever you're going, but I'd recommend you try to get it done in the next month or so."

I seethed that this doctor could be so blasé. I'd shown her the spot on my leg six months earlier and she'd simply shrugged and said it was nothing to worry about. Now she was treating it like an emergency. A later dermatologist tried to tell me that the Eugene dermatologist had probably been right, that the lesion had probably been benign when she first saw it and had then "gone active" in the past six months. I wasn't convinced, especially considering this was my third time around with a squamous cell carcinoma.

We scheduled a month's reservation in an RV park in Coarsegold, California, which was about halfway between Eugene and Desert Hot Springs, and I scheduled an appointment with a dermatologist in nearby Fresno. I thought it hysterical that I found a dermatologist with the surname of Kardashian. I wouldn't be laughing for long though.

If I'd have any inkling of the complicated medical issue that would arise from my little Mohs procedure, I would have possibly embarrassed myself beyond redemption with a full-fledged temper tantrum that would have put a two-year-old to shame. Although I'd speculated that eventually the transmission would fall out of the RV, I hadn't really believed it would happen. Was my metaphor about to come true?

CHAPTER 4

I Do Not Have Cancer

"What'd you find out?"

Michael had just returned from the RV park office to ask about an extension for our reservation. It was mid-December 2021, and I was almost two months post-op from the Mohs surgery that had removed a squamous cell carcinoma from my left leg, just a few inches above my ankle.

"Lady in the office said, 'no problem,' there's no way they'd kick out someone with cancer right before Christmas," he said.

"But I don't have cancer. Why would she say that?"

Michael looked at me with an incredulous expression. "Remember that surgical wound on your leg that won't heal, the one that's keeping us here long after we should be gone? That's cancer." He glared at me as if I was an idiot.

"I had cancer, Michael, and *had* is the operative word. The doctor removed it, and now I don't have cancer anymore." This was so obvious to me, and I didn't understand why my husband couldn't see it.

Michael let out an exasperated sigh and rolled his eyes. "You dodo. You're a cancer patient."

Me, a cancer patient? A dermatologist in Eugene had diagnosed a squamous cell carcinoma on my shin, and then another dermatologist in Fresno had cut it out. The nasty lesion had been cancerous, not me.

Like an unending mantra, the words 'I do not have cancer' looped through my mind. Skin cancer didn't surprise me. I have a fair complexion and have lived most of my life in sunny Florida. When I was growing up, no one knew that ultraviolet rays caused cancer, and it was not until I reached my thirties that researchers got around to developing sunscreen. I'd been doomed from the start, as were most people of my generation. My sense was that skin cancers in old coots were as common as wearing glasses or hearing aids. This was my third bout of this crap, although the first two surgeries had been nothing but shoulder shrugging events. I'll admit the word 'Mohs' created an element of concern, plus this lesion looked nastier than the first two.

Besides which, skin cancer wasn't real cancer. If I were a breast cancer survivor who'd suffered multiple medical intrusions, surgeries, and treatments, I'd look at someone with skin cancer claiming to be a cancer patient with disdain, like some kind of deluded imposter.

🛺

I expected the surgery to be routine, but it was worse than I'd anticipated.

"Once you've had a squamous cell carcinoma, you're at a much higher risk of getting it again," Dr. Kardashian, my dermatologist in Fresno, had said while reviewing my biopsy report from Eugene. "I don't like the size of this thing or how long it's been there. We'll get you scheduled ASAP." I left her office a few minutes later with an appointment for surgery the following Wednesday.

During the surgical procedure, my doctor talked about various skin cancers. "The melanomas are the most serious because they metastasize so quickly. Basal cell cancers aren't so bad since they can typically be diagnosed just from looking at them, and they're usually caught early on."

Lying on the table, I felt an occasional tug on my leg. "The squamous cell carcinomas are harder to diagnose because there's no standard surface appearance. They could be moles, flaky little areas, or red lesions or irritations like the one you had. Regardless of what they look like, they can be very dangerous, go deep, and spread fast."

I had heard of Mohs surgery but had not known until now what it entailed. During a Mohs procedure, the doctor cuts out the visibly abnormal skin and then reviews it microscopically to look for cancer cells around the edges. The idea is to keep removing larger and larger areas around the edges until the microscope image shows no abnormality. Each incision takes about five to ten minutes, and the doctor then sends images of each sample to a laboratory for analysis.

My doctor had several other Mohs surgeries going on that day and left me lying on the table for an hour or more between each incision. It was like being on an assembly line, only with the physician being on the conveyor belt rather than the patient. During the periods while I waited for the doctor's return, I tried to imagine all those other patients also waiting. Did they imagine worst-case scenarios for their futures, as I found myself doing?

After the third extraction of tissue, Dr. Kardashian returned and said, "Your margins are clear. The nurse will move you to a different room so we can sew you up."

"Am I going to need a graft?" I asked. Because the lesion had been in an area with no excess skin, the doctor had mentioned earlier that she might need to take a graft from the inside of my thigh.

"Won't know until I start figuring out how to close it up," she said.

The nurse situated me on a table in a room down the hall, and I mustered the courage to peek at my leg. When I saw the three-inch crater that looked at least half an inch deep, I felt the blood drain from my face. I collapsed flat on my back on the table and a cold sweat erupted on my face. I was sorry I'd looked.

Dr. Kardashian was able to stretch and create a flap of skin from the surrounding area to cover the incision. "I am so glad," she said. "If I'd had to do a graft, you'd have had two incisions to heal and a lot more pain."

I remembered my friend Don from Texas who loved talking about his many Mohs surgeries and skin grafts. "I'm sure I've got a piece of my butt stuck on my nose," he'd say to anyone who'd listen.

The doctor removed her surgical gloves and said, "My nurse will bandage you up." I tamped down a surge of intestinal queasiness, relieved that my ordeal was almost over.

I sat up and dared a look at the ugly, ragged four-inch line of black stitches running somewhat horizontal to my tibia. I quickly plopped back down to a prone position, again with beads of cold sweat popping out on my forehead. I didn't watch as the nurse smothered the incision with antibiotic ointment and wrapped it in several layers of bandages.

My earlier biopsies and squamous cell carcinomas had been quick and easy, with no pain and with the stitches removed a couple of weeks later. I'd assumed this procedure would be the same. Although my doctor had said during the first appointment that healing would take about six weeks, I didn't believe her. Three weeks at most for me, I'd thought.

Now, two months after the surgery, I was on my third prescription for antibiotics and the third different bandaging protocol. My doctor continued to say, "I want you on bed rest with your leg elevated. If this doesn't heal properly, you could be looking at years of long-term wound care management."

I vowed to be a better patient despite how much I hated my current situation. I'd do almost anything to make my husband stop calling me a cancer patient.

I'd also do almost anything to make this damned surgical incision heal.

CHAPTER 5
The Transmission Tumbles

I had always assumed the RV gods would give us a bit of notice when it was time for us to change our lifestyle. In retrospect, I realized the gods had indeed given us adequate notice, but we hadn't been listening. I'd been waiting for something big, such as a heart attack or a stroke, or even a horrific traffic accident that damaged our rig or car. Any number of catastrophes might have grounded us. Although I was still nursing a minor surgical wound, it wasn't infected, and it didn't hurt. As it turned out, my stubborn Mohs wound would have only a minor role with our screeching halt to full-time RVing.

We had spent over four months in California, waiting for my Fresno dermatologist to pronounce my wound healed enough for travel. It was now March of 2022 and too late to go to Desert Hot Springs for the winter as we had planned to do. We opted to head north to Eugene. We'd catch up on all our six-month follow-ups with doctors and then continue north for another summer on the Olympic Peninsula.

Lucky for us, we had grown to like Eugene. While wading through multiple medical appointments, we started spending several late afternoons a week at a nearby wine bar. We'd sit on the large front porch, enjoying a cool breeze and looking at a beautiful little park on the other side of the street. We began meeting and chatting with others, and we became members of the wine club to hang out with our new friends.

We also ventured to other places in town, most often in pursuit of live music, which Eugene offered in abundance. We began to get to know a few of the musicians and travelled around town to hear them play at different venues, usually breweries or wineries. We loved that most of the live music was during later afternoon hours, usually from six to eight p.m. As old geezers, we appreciated getting home before dark.

We went to the Arboretum at Mt. Pisgah two or three times a week for long hikes. We loved Eugene's food trucks, the city's embrace of diversity, the ease of getting across town in less than fifteen minutes with no traffic jams. And, important for folks our ages, we liked and trusted our medical providers, which now included a general practitioner, a podiatrist, a dermatologist, a wound care nurse, a pulmonologist, and a dentist. Before long, we'd add a physical therapist, a diabetes nutrition specialist, an endodontist, and a urologist to our growing list of medical care providers. Reaching our seventies was proving both challenging and a bit unnerving. How many things could go wrong? I sensed the list was theoretically infinite.

Still, we felt like things were going smoothly . . . until our general practitioner threw Michael a major whammy. "I'm going to want to see you every three months from now on," she told him. "And I want you to start physical therapy for the neuropathy in your feet. Better plan on at least three months for the PT." A bombshell could not have startled us more.

By this point in our travels, we'd RVed in every state except Hawaii. That we loved Eugene made our screeching halt easier, and we didn't second-guess our decision to make it our forever home. That term 'forever home' made me chuckle. At our ages, we weren't talking about many years at all.

We viewed Eugene as a Goldilocks kind of town—not too big and not too little, not too hot and not too cold, not too young and not too old. We loved that it was an aging hippie town in some ways but a vibrant young people's mecca in others because of the university. Eugene embraced liberal politics and diversity while simultaneously tolerating staunch conservative and radical views from every direction. Lacking any major industry (Nike had moved its factory further north closer to Port-land), the downtown area contained myriad venues for live music, the-ater, and art. Plus, we always got a kick when we saw balding, gray-haired old men with thin ponytails wearing tie-dyed t-shirts and Birkenstocks sitting in wheelchairs in our neighborhood WinCo supermarket.

We reconciled ourselves to our changed circumstances. "Guess we need to find a place to live," Michael said.

"I don't really care, as long as it has a yard so I can get dirt under my fingernails again." Inwardly, I quivered in excitement. I was getting the house I'd realized a year earlier that I wanted.

CHAPTER 6

What Have We Done?

"I'm not sure I'm ready for this," I'd said as we signed the closing documents for our new house in the Spring Hill Manufactured Home Park. "I never thought this is where I'd end up as an old woman." I felt too young to be moving into an over-55 development despite being seventy-four. Plus, coming from the deep South where poverty and substandard housing proliferated, I couldn't help but think of this manufactured home park as a trailer park. (Here's hoping God and my neighbors will forgive me for saying that.)

Neither wanting nor needing a large house, pool, and yard again, a neighborhood like this made sense to us when we realized we had to settle down. I raged that our motorhome had lasted longer than our bodies. The damn RV was supposed to keep rolling until the transmission hit the ground, and it was also supposed to keep us young and vibrant.

Once we signed the closing documents, even more misgivings popped up. We looked around the neighborhood and wondered if we'd made a huge mistake. All the gingerbread-looking houses in pastel colors with Candyland gumball-shaped trees and shrubs did not look like a place I belonged.

Michael mourned the loss of our RVing lifestyle and would have lived on the road forever had his health allowed. In contrast, I had thought I was ready to settle down in one place and could hardly wait to start digging and planting. Still, as we watched some of our new neighbors trudging down the sidewalk with their canes and walkers, I wondered if maybe we were a bit too young to have moved into this place. Our choice now seemed like a rather drastic, premature step to have taken.

The community did not feel friendly, and I cringed at the way folks looked right through us. The artificially sculpted balls and cubes of foliage in the yards worried me, for this is not the kind of gardening I did. I feared my neighbors would all be grumpy old people with nothing better to do than complain about every little blade of grass that might not be exactly the right height, and I wanted my yard to be a wild, overgrown jungle filled with native plants. It was unfair to immediately assume these folks would complain about my yard, since we'd not yet heard anyone complain about anything. Plus, Michael and I were clearly in the age bracket of folks who belonged in this place. I needed to grow up and accept my age.

Not long after we moved in, Michael had a run-in with one of the long-term residents, Joe. The spat was over our RV, which we'd left overnight in the clubhouse parking lot after returning from a weeklong trip to the coast. A detailer was cleaning our rig, and we planned to return the rig to our storage site as soon as the detailer finished his work.

One of the many rules in our leasing agreement (we owned our house but leased the land) said that owners could leave their RVs in the parking lot for one night only. Joe thought our rig had been there two nights, when it had only been there for one. He was also upset that our detailer was using water from a clubhouse faucet.

According to Michael, Joe went ballistic and accosted him by the mailboxes. "You are not allowed to leave your RV in that parking lot more than one night."

"I didn't," Michael said. "It was there last night, and I plan to take it back to storage today, as soon as the detailer finishes."

"And you can't use park water to wash your RV. It's in the bylaws—it's not allowed."

"The manager gave me permission," Michael said. I wasn't there, but Michael assured me he was being extremely polite so he wouldn't agitate Joe any further.

"Was that from Derek?" Joe practically screamed his anger. "Well, we have a new manager now, and her name is Jill." Unfortunately, this exchange between Joe and Michael was unfolding just one day after Derek, the manager we knew and who had become Michael's friend, had packed up his desk and left after the California corporation that owned the park had fired him.

"Joe, Derek gave me permission to use the park's water, but when I heard Derek was leaving, I made a point of introducing myself to Jill and explaining the situation. Jill gave me permission to use the clubhouse water." Michael paused, reporting to me that he felt rather tense himself at this point. "So, Six Gun Joe, you need to put your pistols back in your holster and head on back home."

I wish I could have heard this conversation. According to Michael, there were five or six people congregated at the mailboxes, and they all overhead the exchange. Per Michael, they all stood there without saying a word as Michael turned away to walk home.

While we weren't so sure about our new neighborhood and its residents, we were pleasantly surprised at how comfortable, spacious, and well-designed we found our new "double-wide." If one counted the garage, it was a triple-wide. "This definitely works," Michael said. After living in an RV for almost three years, our 1,637 sq.-ft. living quarters felt decadent and obscene.

Spring Hill was a community of 102 homes; most of the over-55 developments in Eugene had several hundred. We liked the smaller size of our neighborhood and didn't mind that it lacked a pool, jacuzzi and spa, tennis and pickleball courts, and other amenities that some of the other communities offered. Ours had an exercise room, a library with a billiards table, a huge kitchen, and a large open area with tables and chairs for meetings, potlucks, and other gatherings.

McMansions surrounded our little park, and we assumed buying here would be a good financial investment. "Who would have approved manufactured homes in a zip code like this?" I had asked. Later I learned that the manufactured homes came first and the upscale McMansions second. Still, the corporate owners of Spring Hill Park had a lengthy application process for membership and an obsession with enforcing the rules for how owners had to keep their houses and yards. Another positive aspect to our purchase was no concern that anyone would ever mistake this community for a trailer park.

Derek, the park manager, had told us that many residents seldom left their homes, which I had found depressing and hard to believe. Within a couple of months, however, I believed what he'd said. At some addresses, the only activities seemed to be rideshare vans coming to transport folks for medical appointments, adult children and grandchildren dropping in occasionally, and a sporadic housekeeper coming to clean.

I winced at the number of first responder vehicles coming into the park—firetrucks, ambulances, and an occasional police cruiser. Noting the absence of sirens and blinking lights, we were somewhat reassured when neighbors told us these were mostly safety checks rather than emergencies.

On a positive note, I loved how my new life in Spring Hill made me feel so young. Within a couple of weeks, I'd upped my pace, put a bit more bounce in my step, and straightened my spine to stand taller as I took my daily walks. I knew that it was probably relative, but I could already see advantages of being among the youngest and healthiest in the neighborhood.

Maybe this metaphorical failed transmission would work out for us after all. We could keep the RV and continue to travel, but not for months on end as we'd done before. Hopefully from this point forward, Michael would be reasonable about how long each RV road trip would last and I wouldn't have to return home to plant catastrophes. And maybe someday, we'd even get back to the Olympic Peninsula.

CHAPTER 7

It's a Wonderful Day in the Neighborhood

"I'm Eleanor, and I live next door."

I jumped at the sound of a faint voice behind me. I turned and faced a tiny, frail woman who weighed seventy pounds at most with her hair wet. I was on my side of the fence that separated my yard from my next-door neighbor's, using a plant app on my phone to identify the unfamiliar foliage in my yard. Startled, I introduced myself and explained what I was doing.

"Oh, those aren't your plants. They're mine. Here's where the property line is," she said and gestured with her hand. "The fence is mine, but you'll have to keep your side clean." She paused. "Actually, this grass here is mine, too, up to about here." She pointed, marking an area at least two feet from the fence. "The previous owners mowed it though." I noticed a smug smile as she shared this information.

I hated white vinyl fences, and every single house in Spring Hill had one. I wanted to plant fast-growing shrubs along the property lines and hide every square inch of that shiny ugly fence. I didn't tell Eleanor, but I had no intention of ever washing a vinyl fence, regardless of whose property it was on.

"Who takes care of this flower bed?" I asked, gesturing toward the overgrown area where I'd been pointing my phone trying to identify

24

the jungle of plants squeezed into the bed. The area was a mess—thick with four and five-foot-tall, sickly-yellowish plants, an aggressive ground cover, and a thick undergrowth of what looked like weeds.

"I used to, but I haven't been able to do much gardening lately."

The bed looked like no one had touched it in years, and unfortunately, this was the view from our living room window. I'd already started planning how I'd make the area beautiful so I wouldn't wince every time I looked out. "Then you won't mind it I spruce it up some?"

"You go right ahead." As Eleanor turned to go, she glanced back and said, "But you might want to take care of the green algae on the fence first. It's pretty bad."

My curiosity and wonder over all these new-to-me plants evaporated. I'd looked at enough plants for one day, and I'd also met enough new neighbors. If I'd dreamed of becoming best friends with my new next-door neighbor, Eleanor had just smashed that dream to hell. What a crochety old woman, I remembered thinking. Already bossing me around and telling me I'd be responsible for the care of plants on her property. Where was the 'welcome to the neighborhood' or 'it's nice to meet you'?

In time, I'd realize that closing the blinds in my living room and blocking the view was a totally satisfactory solution to the problem.

Michael and I settled in rather quickly, or at least we thought so at first. We found two couples in the neighborhood who were members of our nearby wine club, though their enthusiasm for adult beverages didn't approach our near-insatiable levels. We became friends with a single woman two doors down who'd moved in just four months before us. We got to know a couple of former Peace Corps volunteers who shared our excitement about getting out and taking part in community activities. And I found several women in the neighborhood whose passion for gardening approximated mine.

However, the percentage of widows I met sobered and scared me. Was there something in the drinking water that killed off all the men? Of course not, but I soon realized I'd have a lot of sisterly support in this community if I outlasted Michael.

"I'm pretty sure," I said to Michael, "that out of all these houses, we'll find more friends before long."

"Next spring, when the weather gets better and folks are outside again," my husband said. We had moved into Spring Hill in September. The days were getting shorter, and soon the rainy season would begin. Folks had warned us that Eugene winters could be long, dark, and wet with many folks going into hibernation. I couldn't see Michael and me doing that, though. The pandemic had eased, and after almost three years of social and pandemic isolation as RVers, we wanted to meet people, develop friends, and go out into the community. Our nearby wine bar planned to open an inside lounge and promised live music three or four times a week. Would we dare go inside an enclosed room like that after all our fears of dying from Covid? Michael and I looked at each other and found ourselves in total agreement. At this point in our lives, we'd take the risk.

One of our first surprises about Spring Hill was the high turnover. For Sale signs popped up on a regular basis. Existing residents moved out and new folks moved in. Occasionally someone would post a sign on the community bulletin board of a resident's death and information about the upcoming memorial service. Every few weeks, we saw an adult child yank an aging parent or two out of Spring Hill and move them into assisted living facilities or nursing homes. Within a month of moving in, Michael and I were no longer the new kids on the block. This revolving door opened and closed at a dizzying pace. I felt a bit unnerved.

I attended my first 'estate sale' in the neighborhood, an event in which contracted estate managers displayed every item in the home with a price written on a round sticker dot. Offerings included items like rusted baking sheets, half-filled bottles of ten-year-old aspirin, threadbare linens, and more crocheted doilies than I could count. I winced as I watched hordes of people descend like vultures, sometimes almost grabbing items out of each other's hands. I'd later cringe at my own participation in this public exposure of such intimate items of daily living that had belonged to an elderly couple, one recently deceased and the other no longer able to live alone. I hoped my focus on potted plants and gardening supplies at the sale would somehow exonerate my complicity in violating the privacy of these former neighbors.

I'd always prided myself on being flexible and willing to adjust to whatever the future brought. I'd undergone a couple of huge transitions in the past decade. The first was retiring from forty years of work, and the second was becoming a full-time RVer after decades of home ownership and enthusiastic gardening. In the past year, we'd faced Michael's gradual but unrelenting medical issues that demanded we find a home base with excellent medical care.

In other ways, however, moving into Spring Hill felt like the greatest lifestyle challenge I'd ever faced. There was nothing quite like seeing the folks who lived around me carted off to hospitals, assisted living facilities, and morgues. I'd never seen changes like this before, and my new neighborhood afforded me a catbird's view. It was a wakeup call I couldn't pretend not to hear.

I realized I needed to rethink this wonderful day in the neighborhood perception. Yes, folks took immaculate care of their homes. Sprinkler systems ran in every yard several times a week during the summers, and lawn care guys descended daily like swarms of angry bees to mow, prune, shape, and correct any leaf or blade that dared misbehave.

My early encounters with Eleanor triggered pangs of anxiety. Did I belong in a community of such old, old people? I'd never had such a deep immersion in a group of seniors before, and I wasn't sure I liked it despite the recognition that I was seventy-four years old and not getting any younger, no matter how much I might have wished I were. I could only hope that in time I would adjust and stop being so hysterical.

CHAPTER 8

Not All Cancers are Created Equal

Doctors diagnosed my friend Norma Jean with colorectal cancer six months after my skin cancer surgery. When Norma Jean told me she had cancer, I shuddered with chagrin that I'd made such a big deal over my small skin lesion. And irritated anew that my husband would dare say I had cancer when my best RV buddy had just received a Real McCoy diagnosis from a large team of oncologists and gastroenterologists.

It's easy to remember the day Norma Jean realized she had a problem—May 24th, 2022. She woke up hemorrhaging and had been rushed to the emergency room. She and her husband Jeremy were full-time RVers and were in an RV park in Hondo, Texas, about forty miles west of San Antonio. With a population of just over eight thousand, Hondo had a small, twenty-five bed critical care hospital and not much else.

Within minutes of examining Norma Jean in the ER, the doctor ordered an ambulance to take her to a large hospital in San Antonio.

"I wasn't in this ER more than ten minutes waiting for that ambulance when all hell broke loose," Norma Jean told me on the phone a couple of hours later. "You realize that Hondo is about midway between San Antonio and Uvalde, don't you?"

"Oh my god. Uvalde, where a man just shot all those children?" I'd gotten a news alert on my cell phone earlier, and Michael and I had glued ourselves to CNN.

"There were people screaming and crying, doors slamming, sirens wailing, just chaos like you wouldn't believe," Norma Jean said. "Someone, I have no idea who, came into the ER and announced there'd been a shooting in Uvalde and that those victims were taking priority over everything and everybody else."

Norma Jean and I chatted for a couple more minutes as she bided time, waiting for her chariot to arrive. Jeremy was with her, and she didn't want to run her phone battery down. She later told me a doctor had rushed into her room at one point, looked at her, and burst out crying. Occasionally nurses would pop in to apologize for the delays, saying there was nothing they could do other than try to keep the shooting victims alive until ambulances could take them to area trauma centers.

As it turned out, Norma Jean lay on a gurney in the Hondo emergency room for over eight hours waiting for an ambulance. Jeremy begged the hospital to let him drive her to San Antonio, but the hospital refused to release her. "We're not letting a hemorrhaging patient walk out of here," hospital personnel told him. "The liability is too great. Besides which, these shooting victims have filled all the ERs within a hundred square miles. There's no place that would see your wife right now even if we had an ambulance."

"Want to hear something ironic?" Norma Jean texted me the next morning. She was finally in a room in a San Antonio hospital. "I've been trying to get a colonoscopy referral from my primary care physician for almost two years, telling him I thought something was wrong, and he just kept saying I worried too much and that it wasn't yet time. Looks like I'm finally going to get that colonoscopy." She ended with a smiley-face emoji.

Norma Jean and I texted back and forth several times that day. In my friend's inimitable style, she joked about her love of colonoscopies and how much she looked forward to finally getting another one after an almost three-year wait.

The biopsy results came the following day. "They found multiple polyps, and they're all malignant," my friend wrote in her text to me. The following day, Jeremy sent a group email to family and friends saying that doctors had diagnosed Norma Jean with Stage 3 colorectal cancer and were developing a treatment plan. He described the cancer as "very treatable."

"You're just trying to outdo me," I joked to my friend. "Colon cancer trumps skin cancer any day of the week."

We both chuckled.

By this time in our nomadic travels, Michael and I had left the Sierra foothills and landed in Eugene, Oregon for routine medical care, which we referred to as our 70,000-mile tune-ups, since we were both in our seventies. We planned to stay a couple of months and then head further north.

My first order of business in Eugene was to see a wound care specialist, an appointment I'd scheduled long before we left California. My stubborn squamous cell carcinoma surgical wound wasn't healing.

"I'm worried about you," Norma Jean said. "Think there might still be cancer in there that's keeping it from healing?"

"How can you possibly be worried about me? You're about to start chemo and radiation. All I'm having to do is apply Betadine and keep the damn thing covered." I couldn't believe my friend would be worrying about me when she was facing grueling four-day-a-week treatments. I wondered how I would have dealt with a diagnosis like hers. I'd always put skin cancer in the same category as acne or eczema—unsightly sometimes, but certainly not life-threatening. But what if she was right about cancer still being in my leg?

Doctors had inserted a port in Norma Jean's chest in which to inject the chemo with a large needle. Each Monday, they'd put in the needle, and each Thursday they'd take it out. "That needle is the size of a huge nail," she reported. "I can't even describe how painful it is when that thing gets hammered in each week."

I cringed at the image and experienced a fleeting wave of nausea.

The San Antonio hospital where Norma Jean received treatment was only forty-five miles from Hondo, but the trip took at least an hour and a half each way because of traffic and construction. She endured the radiation with no side effects, describing it as "a piece of cake." In contrast, within a couple of weeks, the chemo began taking its toll. Nausea set in, and the drive into the hospital sparked motion sickness, making the queasiness worse.

About halfway through the first three-month treatment regime, doctors wanted to do another colonoscopy to see if the tumors had shrunk.

"Oh, you're so lucky," Michael said to Norma Jean during one of our frequent Zoom calls. "I can only hope I'll get to go under again before too much longer." In the past couple of months, Michael had been under anesthesia three times with dental, optical, and urological procedures. It'd become an ongoing joke between him and Norma Jean over who could accumulate the most amount of time knocked out by doctors.

"I'm sort of looking forward to this one," Norma Jean said the day before her appointment. "At least I'll be under anesthesia for a few minutes and won't have to think about this damn port and how much I hate chemo."

Later she told me about her conversation with the anesthesiologist when she woke up from the procedure. "How long did you keep me under this time?" she'd asked.

"Less than three minutes."

"That wasn't near long enough. Next time I expect you to do better."

🛺

I minimized my concern about my recalcitrant wound whenever Norma Jean asked about it. How could I possibly whine about such a piddly little thing when my closest friend faced a foe as formidable as The Big C?

"I hope you're exaggerating about those ulcers on your leg," Norma Jean would text. "I think you ought to get a second opinion."

Perhaps from guilt, fear, or my own psycho-hysteria, I began to experience sympathetic symptoms with my friend. Her back would hurt; my back would hurt. She'd feel queasy; I'd feel a bit queasy. Her butt hurt; my butt began to hurt.

"Think I'm catching your cancer electronically?" I joked with her in texts.

"Not a laughing matter," Norma Jean said. "You need a colonoscopy. Go to your doctor and demand one."

"I think my doctor will tell me it's not time." I felt lame as I said it. Norma Jean had badgered her primary care physician to refer her for a colonoscopy, and he refused. If he'd ordered the damn thing two years earlier when she'd first asked, they might have found the cancer earlier and she might not be going through these invasive, barbaric intrusions into her body. I alternated between thinking I should take her advice about requesting a referral for one and feeling I was a hypochondriacal maniac.

The bottom line was that I didn't want another opinion; I didn't think I could handle any more bad news. While our old bodies still functioned okay, doctors were finding new issues in both me and my husband every time new lab results arrived. Nothing serious, just something else doctors wanted to watch.

Being in an over-55 community turned up the volume on every lab result value that wavered. I couldn't shake the feeling that I saw my future with every cane or walker that passed by my front kitchen window. The pandemic had taken a toll on us, and we had only recently dared to go into restaurants after not doing so for over two years. Then we both caught Covid, though luckily our cases were mild. But if anything was making me a bit psycho, it was this frigging surgical wound that wouldn't heal.

"I'm having all these sympathetic symptoms with Norma Jean, and I'm not sure it's healthy," I said to Michael one day.

"That's crazy. What are you talking about?"

"Norma Jean's become my one daily, consistent contact with the outside world. We met almost three years ago and have only seen each other a handful of times since then. How did she end up becoming my best friend?"

"You two connected."

"I guess. When we took off in the RV, I could never have imagined a pandemic erupting and changing everything. It made us travel like reclusive introverts rather than the vivacious, gregarious nomads I'd imagined us being."

"That helps to explain what brought you and Norma Jean together, but the reasons aren't even important. Caring about your friend is what counts," Michael said, "although I agree that your sympathetic symptoms are a bit bizarre."

After about two months of chemo and radiation, on one of their rough, bouncing rides back to their RV park from the hospital, Norma Jean texted me, "I'm considering opting out of treatment and just living till I die. Jeremy's not happy with that."

Norma Jean's next colonoscopy results were not good. The doctors reported that while the tumors in the colon appeared to have shrunk, the cancer may have spread outside the intestines. Doctors wanted more tests before starting another round of chemo and radiation.

In the four months from the first diagnosis until now, Norma Jean had disintegrated from an optimistic, spunky woman into a depressed, pain-wracked patient. During one Zoom call, she said to us, "The cancer didn't really surprise me, but I never thought I'd get the kind that hurt so bad." I marveled that my friend was able to keep her sense of humor. I laughed with her, but on the inside, my heart cried.

Doctors scheduled another colonoscopy as well as other tests. "By the time my treatments are done," she quipped, "I'm going to miss people sticking things up my butt." I was glad we were texting now rather than Zooming. I didn't want Norma Jean to see my tears.

"You'll just have to ignore Jeremy for a while," Norma Jean said a couple of days later. "He's not ready to face reality yet. He still thinks I can beat this thing."

"Maybe you can." My words rang hollow, even to me. I hated myself for saying something to my friend that I didn't believe. It felt placating, and facing death should not be a situation to sugarcoat. Backtracking to redeem myself from disingenuousness, I said, "I can only imagine how excruciating this must be for him." Those words rang true. I hoped my friend would understand that I meant her husband perhaps needed to hang on to hope even more than she did. She was the one on a journey. He'd be the one left behind. If I thought I felt helpless, I could only imagine how Jeremy must feel.

The day prior to a scheduled scan of her liver, Norma Jean woke up with paralysis in her legs. Doctors prioritized a scan of her spine, which showed multiple tumors along the vertebrae and at the base of the skull. Doctors wheeled her into surgery the following day to remove the tumors.

A week later, with my friend still flat on her back, the hospital in San Antonio ordered her transferred to a rehab facility in Hondo. Except the transport deposited her in a nursing home in Castroville, a small town twenty miles from Hondo in a facility that did not offer physical therapy.

Details of my friend's rapid deterioration are muddy, murky, and macabre. A bed finally opened in rehab in Hondo three days before Thanksgiving. I wired a large Autumn flower arrangement in a basket, but by this time, Norma Jean was so sick she hardly acknowledged the flowers. Although we would exchange more text messages, I didn't know at the time that I would never have another playful, hopeful, funny text, telephone, or Zoom exchange with her again. Ever.

My near-daily texting with Norma Jean ended in mid-December when things took yet more turns for the worse. Numbness returned in her legs, and doctors performed another spinal surgery. The chemo port in her chest became infected, and she became delirious and lost contact with reality. I winced at how blithely I had joked about becoming a psycho when my friend had lost contact with reality because of a raging infection.

After the infection resolved and Norma Jean "returned to herself," her pain increased exponentially. My last text communication with her was on December 21st when she texted that they'd taken her by ambulance from Hondo to San Antonio for her first radiation treatment in over three months. She wrote, "It was a very big deal being in so much pain."

My heart was breaking. I'd been busy baking cookies for the holidays, and I decided to send a batch to her. On December 21st, I boxed up about two dozen and shipped them by FedEx, who promised a December 23rd delivery date. Just in time for Christmas, I thought.

As if my body sensed my friend's impending death, my Mohs surgical wound re-opened on December 22nd. It had been four months since my wound care nurse pronounced the incision healed and closed my case. The timing felt eerie, especially as I recalled the many parallel sympathetic symptoms I'd experienced during the past seven months of Norma Jean's illness. It was uncanny.

Norma Jean slipped out of consciousness on December 24th following an injection of pain medication. She never regained consciousness and peacefully crossed over on December 27th. Jeremy was in the room with her as she took her last breath.

🛺

My mother had passed away in 2006. She and I had been very close, emailing each other four or five times each week and speaking on the phone every Sunday. About two years after she passed, I opened my email one morning and saw an email from her that had appeared in my inbox a couple of hours earlier. My shock was indescribable. I called Comcast Communications in Ft. Myers, Florida at once and demanded an explanation. I knew my mother was dead, for I'd seen her take her last breath and was by her side as her body cooled. I still had her remains, decades later, on the top shelf of a closet because I couldn't yet bear to say goodbye. How could I suddenly get an email from her? Comcast explained the email as a computer glitch.

I didn't believe dead souls could send electronic communications to folks left behind. It just couldn't happen. Still, I found myself for weeks after Norma Jean's passing looking at the text icon on my cell phone multiple times a day, hoping to see an alert. I longed for a reality glitch that would find my friend still alive.

I study my Mohs surgical wound daily, wondering if Norma Jean might have been right about it still being cancerous. My Eugene dermatologist said no, unequivocally not, visibly irritated that I'd second-guessed his opinion. Norma Jean had tried to tell her doctor that she thought she might have colon cancer, and he repeatedly dismissed her requests for a colonoscopy for two years. Am I foolish to accept my doctor's visual assessment that I don't have a squamous cell carcinoma on my leg anymore? If I asked him to do a biopsy, I'm sure he'd bark out a definitive negative response.

I tried a different tact and went to my primary care physician, who reacted differently, not to my stubborn Mohs surgical wound but to my report of a sore butt. She referred me to a gastroenterologist who scheduled a colonoscopy. I'd obviously imagined my butt pain, for the gastroenterologist found nothing of concern. I'm sorry Norma Jean is not here for me to tell her the results, or for her to congratulate me for finally getting a turn under anesthesiology.

My body hurts somewhere every time I think of my friend. This was the first time I'd taken a cancer journey with someone, and I was horrified at what a barbaric, unrelenting, and unforgiving disease it is. I'm appalled that there is so much muddling and bungling in modern-day medical care. But even as I remember all my psycho-pseudo sympathetic cancer symptoms, and even as I think that maybe Norma Jean and I both had and have a bit of psychic witchy-ness in us, I stand by my original assertion to Michael: I am not a cancer patient. I had a cancer, which a doctor removed, and now I'm just a run-of-the-mill wound care patient who'll probably die with a gaping ulcer on her leg.

In the meantime, I do not have cancer.

But if I did have cancer, I'm in a good place to die in this over-55 community. If a terminal illness popped up in our house, I'm thinking my elderly neighbors would embrace Michael and me with comforting but realistic sentiments. When I consider the concentration of old coots in Spring Hill, I'm betting there's a wealth of medical horror stories that theoretically could be shared. If I die first, I'm feeling pretty sure that at least a couple of the widow-women here would reach out and bring casseroles to my grieving husband. At least he wouldn't be left as a bitter old man hitting on women in an RV park laundry room somewhere. I'd like to think I'm wrong, that perhaps there are some nice older women out there who really might enjoy having a man around. Maybe there's even one right here in Spring Hill who'd take care of my husband.

CHAPTER 9

Eleanor Moves On

We moved into our new home in early September when the weather was hot and the air thick with wildfire smoke. By October, the weather was cooler and cleaner, and I started seeing more of Eleanor when she'd come outside to walk her dog, a Chihuahua that appeared to mirror her age and frailty. If I was out front gardening, Eleanor would stop to talk. During one of our sidewalk chats, Eleanor told me she'd turned ninety-one years old the previous July.

Michael and I both enjoyed cooking. After years of cramped RV kitchen challenges, we embraced our huge new kitchen with unbridled enthusiasm. I went on a cookie-baking spree in late October, planning to fill the freezer with sweets for the holidays.

After an afternoon of baking Toll House Cookies, I glanced out to see Eleanor walking home from the mailboxes. I grabbed a baggie and three cookies and ran outside to catch her before she reached her front steps. During the past two months, I'd gotten to know Eleanor a bit. While I wouldn't say I was fond of her, I was learning more about her and beginning to be concerned. Plus, I was in awe over her age.

I couldn't remember having ever spoken with anyone in their nineties before. Despite her age, Eleanor lived independently and still drove herself to doctor's appointments and the grocery store. Both my parents had passed away in their eighties. I found myself thinking about my own genetic inheritances and actions I could take to prolong my life. I knew my priority should be giving up my beloved red wine, but I didn't think this was going to happen anytime soon, not with my current level of Spring Hill angst.

"Oh, you remembered that I love chocolate." Eleanor smiled when I handed her the cookies. "Now you just hang on a minute. I baked some brownies yesterday, and I want to give you a couple." I protested but to no avail as I watched her slowly make her way up the two steps to her porch and into her house. A couple of minutes later, she returned and handed me a plastic bag.

When I opened the bag in my kitchen a few minutes later, I found it filled with coffee grounds. While Eleanor's confusion could have been one of poor vision, since brownies and coffee grounds are about the same color, I nevertheless had trouble shaking her mistake. I could only imagine the worry I would feel in the months to come for my new next-door neighbor if things like this continued to happen. My social work heart was beginning to bleed over Eleanor's fragility, vulnerability, and confusion.

Hadn't any of the neighbors noticed that this old woman was on the decline? I never saw anyone from the neighborhood ring her front door to check on her or come out to talk with her when she walked her dog or shuffled her way to the mailboxes. But then, I didn't see a lot of folks anywhere in this development spending much time visiting with their neighbors, not on the sidewalks and not anywhere else. Maybe this was why so many of the folks in Spring Hill we'd met seemed aloof and unfriendly towards us. Perhaps there were things about their neighbors, including us, they'd just not want to know and thought it better not to be friendly enough to learn about their neighbors' problems or medical issues.

The dilemma haunted me. If you knew of someone's vulnerability, did it make you responsible to do something to help? I'd spent a forty-year career assuming my job was to support, facilitate, and help in every way possible. I now had a looping tape of worry about Eleanor's welfare running nonstop in my mind. In some ways, I'd have preferred not knowing the few details about Eleanor I already knew.

How many other folks in Spring Hill were this far into the sunset of their years? I tried to imagine becoming friends with people and then watching them deteriorate and die not long afterwards.

Did I really want to develop relationships with these Spring Hill contemporaries? Did I want to cultivate friendships that would remind me daily of my own mortality and impending demise? The thing that upset me the most was realizing that I, at seventy-four, was also an elderly person despite wanting to believe I was still in the prime of my life.

Moving into this over-55 community required a new mindset, and I wasn't sure which attitude and course of action to embrace. Dying as an art form? How would one muster the fortitude and stamina to pull that off? Should I rage against the injustice of aging? Passively acquiesce to the inevitability by withering up and not even trying anymore? Maybe I should ignore my age as well as this community with all its infirmities. Tomorrow I could go right out and buy a motorcycle or take up skydiving. It'd sure be fun to sign up for a round-the-world trip. Perhaps I should just spend every penny of my money and say to hell with it all.

Shortly after Eleanor's brownie mistake, I saw a fire truck in front of her house again. According to neighbors, Eleanor wore a medical alert around her neck which she'd sometimes accidently push, thus triggering a first responder safety check. She had a lockbox on her front door that enabled authorized personnel to enter after punching in a code in the event she didn't answer. During the next couple of months, the frequency of workers arriving in firetrucks, ambulances, and police cruisers increased.

"Did you hear that music in the backyard last night?" Eleanor asked as she shuffled towards me on the sidewalk a couple of weeks following the last fire truck visit. I sweated under the blistering sun and stifling heat of a late October heat wave. Even the smoke from wildfires to the east didn't dampen my enthusiasm for cleaning out the overgrown flower bed between my new home and Eleanor's. I'd accepted Eleanor's admonition that this was my bed to maintain despite her claim that it belonged to her, not me.

"No, I didn't hear a thing," I said.

"I'm surprised. It was really loud. Almost sounded like it was coming through my heart monitor." Eleanor sighed and switched the conversation to ask what I was doing in the flower bed along her fencerow. "The last people who lived in that house kept up this flower bed, too," she said with a chuckle. I wondered what kind of patsy I'd become to maintain my next-door neighbor's flower bed for her.

A few days later, Eleanor rang the doorbell and handed me a small piece of paper. "This is my phone number. I wanted you to have it, and I'd like yours as well."

I invited her in, got an index card, and wrote down the contact information for both me and Michael.

"That's good," Eleanor said when I gave her the numbers. "That music is getting worse, and I'm afraid I'm going to have to call the police if it continues."

My internal alarm moved up another notch, and my social work instincts kicked in. Eleanor needed support, reassurance, and perhaps a bit of monitoring. Surely, she must have family in the area who check in on her, I thought.

The frequency of fire truck visits increased at Eleanor's house, and occasionally, an ambulance or police cruiser also appeared. I learned that Eleanor had two sons who managed assisted living facilities a couple of miles down the road and a granddaughter in nursing school. All three of these family members upped their visitations in what seemed like direct proportion to the increased visitation from responders in uniforms.

Through my now-frequent sidewalk chats with Eleanor, I learned she believed the neighbor who lived behind her, whose backyard also backed up to half of my backyard, was taunting and harassing her. She claimed he climbed her fence at night and played loud music, smoked cigarettes, and partied in her backyard, with the noise keeping her awake. Sometimes she'd call me at ten o'clock at night, asking if I could see or hear anything. I'd dutifully walk outside with the phone and report to Eleanor that my backyard was quiet and that her backyard looked empty as well. Occasionally I'd glance out the window at night and see either law enforcement or paramedics walking along the side of my house towards the back to peek over the fence to look in Eleanor's backyard.

Eleanor's reports turned darker, and she began to talk about being scared. "I think this guy plans to hurt me," she said during one of our phone calls. "I don't know what to do."

"Have you told the police?" I didn't know what else to say, since I couldn't very well tell her the situation was in her mind, not in her backyard.

"Yes, and they said they went over to his house, but they never told me what they found out. I don't think they really went."

Eleanor's complaints became more bizarre. "He can hear everything I say and knows everything I do," she told me. "He's listening to us right now. I think he's got a connection through the registers on the floor." And then on another occasion she said, "It's like he thinks he used to be my boyfriend and he's angry at me for breaking up with him."

"What do your children think about all of this?" I asked.

"They act like they don't believe me."

This went on for a couple of months. Daily, I struggled with my conscience about what I should do. Eleanor had lived here thirty-five years, best as I could figure. I had lived here three months. I felt like I should do something, but no one else, except Polly on the other side of Eleanor, seemed to even notice Eleanor's distress.

Minding one's own business was a value my parents had taught me as a child, and it was possibly one of the reasons they'd been surprised when I chose social work as a career. Social work was all about getting into other people's business, although I mostly had worked in voluntary settings where folks could refuse my help if they didn't want it.

I considered stopping one of Eleanor's sons when he came to her house to express my concern. But as a newbie in the neighborhood, I opted not to. I began to suspect that this was a neighborhood where people stayed out of each other's business, which I found to be a positive thing. Despite all my years in the helping professions, I'd always loved Henry Don Thoreau's quote: "If I knew for a certainty that a man was coming to my house with the conscious design of doing me good, I should run for my life." I felt relieved in some ways that the residents of Spring Hill were minding their own business and staying out of Eleanor's.

Then, one day, the paramedics arrived, and unlike the times before, this time they strapped Eleanor to a gurney, loaded her into the ambulance, and took her away. A neighbor said she'd heard that Eleanor had developed a respiratory infection. Eleanor stayed in the hospital for about a week. Within a couple of weeks of her return home, she was again walking her dog several times a day. "My sons keep telling me I need to go to assisted living," she told me. "I'm not doing it. I don't need that yet."

Polly, the neighbor on the other side of Eleanor, and I had become friends. We talked about Eleanor often and kept each other abreast of developments and our concerns. "Why won't those sons step in and take charge?" I asked Polly one day. "It's horrible hearing her talk about being afraid someone's going to hurt her. No one should live in that kind of fear."

"I've heard the sons have tried but that Eleanor won't do anything they tell her to do."

I thought about this for a while, then laughed. "I hope I'll be like that, too. Good for her."

A For Sale sign went up in Eleanor's front yard in early December. "I don't really plan to sell," she told me. "I'm just seeing what the market is like." While housing prices were dropping and interest rates rising, our sense was that those factors made little difference when it came to senior housing. Spring Hill was a premier manufactured home community, and houses generally sold within a couple of weeks. Michael and I saw Eleanor's realtor showing the property several times the first week it was on the market. Then traffic slowed down.

"I told that realtor to just put things on hold," Eleanor said to me shortly after the lull began. "I'm not ready to do this yet." Then, a week after that, the realtor started showing the house again, so I assumed Eleanor had changed her mind.

Eleanor's house sold in less than a month. She sorted through the 1,900 sq.-ft. house, where she'd lived for over three decades, packing what she wanted to take with her and arranging pickups from St. Vinny's for the things she no longer wanted. She moved into an independent living facility less than two miles from Spring Hill in early March. According to the neighborhood rumor, it was not the place where her family had wanted her to go.

I felt strange about Eleanor moving out just seven months after Michael and I moved in. I had wanted her to move into a safer, less isolated living situation where help would be available twenty-four-hours a day, thus ending the need to call first responders at all hours of the day and night. But when Eleanor actually moved into a safer place, I felt guilty. While I don't believe that hoping for something can make it happen, I nevertheless harbored a bit of culpability that I'd perhaps contributed to Eleanor's deterioration. Should I have told her the neighbor behind her was as nice as he could be and was not in her backyard smoking, playing loud music, and partying every night? Should I have insisted to her that he was not checking her movements, eavesdropping on her phone conversations, or planning to kill her? Despite my social work background, I'd had little experience with geriatric patients with dementia.

I had never imagined a living situation like the one I now found myself in. I'd always lived in neighborhoods where residents ran the gamut from young to old, though I'm positive I'd never had three neighbors, all over the age of ninety, within my line of vision from a kitchen window. I felt chagrined that Eleanor, as the youngest of several nonagenarians in Spring Hill, should have been the first to go. I can only hope she is raising hell in her new independent living facility.

CHAPTER 10

It's Hard to Impress Old People

I became an accidental author when my charming husband sweet-talked me into agreeing to the purchase of an RV. RV travel uprooted me from my Florida home where I'd nurtured 200 orchids and tended an award-winning yard, thus triggering a rather inappropriate snit fit. I don't apologize though. One does not simply go off in an RV and leave plants behind to fend for themselves. My love of plants was such that it felt immoral. Despite the elaborate effort I made to find responsible plant sitters, especially for my orchid collection, I invariably returned home after every trip to find a few casualties.

I might have embarrassed myself irreparably with my immature travel attitude had I not hammered out my conflicted confusion on my laptop. I hadn't wanted to travel and see the country—I wanted to read, eat lunch with friends, and tend to my plants. However, I soon realized that traveling, having new adventures, and writing humorous stories about plunging into the unknown were much more fun than staying in one place. I could read on the road, and we could make new friends and keep in touch with the old ones electronically. I wouldn't be able to do the intense gardening I now enjoyed, but I could hire plant sitters to care for my babies until we settled down again.

RVing stimulated my imagination and gave me things to write about. While on the road, I managed to write three humorous, nonfiction books and have a dozen or so articles published in magazines and journals during the first six years of RVing. When I thought about these writing accomplishments and how I had fulfilled a childhood dream of becoming a writer, I admitted that my husband had been right about an RV changing my life.

During those early months of living in Spring Hill, I realized our little neighborhood was exposing me to yet another world I'd never even considered, just as RVing had done. It shocked me to realize how immersed I was in a community of old people. Not that I ever thought of myself as a nihilist, but when I looked around this over-55 park, the horror of my own death broadsided me. I'm not sure younger people are able to see the realities of aging. I didn't see it even during my sixties, but now that I'm in my seventies, it sometimes seems as if a dark empty end is all that lies ahead.

Before she moved away, Eleanor and I had gotten to know each other somewhat well. At one point, I mentioned being a writer, and Eleanor said she'd love to read one of my books. Thinking it'd be a nice thing to do, a couple of days later I gave her a copy of my first book. This was before she started telling me about the wild parties in her backyard and about the neighbor who listened to her phone conversations through the registers in her house.

Three days later, Eleanor flagged me down on the sidewalk. "I just wanted to tell you how much I loved your book," she said, "but I have a couple of questions. When you and your husband were in Alaska, did you see the aurora borealis?" I answered that question, along with a couple of others. Her questions and comments led me to believe she'd read the entire book. For someone who had confused brownies and coffee grounds, I was super impressed at Eleanor's memory and reading comprehension. I started to think a bit differently about my next-door neighbor.

The conversation with Eleanor reminded me that I'd given copies of my book to several other Spring Hill residents, most of whom I had socialized with over coffee or wine, taken walks with, or chatted with on back patios. I'd considered them friends, since we'd laughed, joked, and found easy conversation. But not one of them had ever mentioned reading my book. Not even one.

Self-doubt and feelings of inadequacy began to haunt. Did all these supposed friends with whom I'd shared my book view me as a fake? A terrible writer? Had they read a few pages and slammed the book shut in boredom or disgust? Or worse yet, were they embarrassed for me? What a boondoggle that ninety-one-year-old Eleanor was the only one in my new neighborhood to tell me she'd read the damn thing.

In time I learned that Eleanor was not Spring Hill's oldest resident. Not by at least six years. Eleanor had a good friend named Winifred who lived diagonally across the street from me, who was ninety-four. I'd gotten to know Winifred through the community garden club. Neighbors told me Winifred loved to garden while listening to big band swing music. She reportedly danced and sang in her backyard as she weeded and pruned.

Winning the oldest award in Spring Hill, however, was ninety-seven-year-old Madeline. Michael had found himself somewhat trapped in the Spring Hill clubhouse one Sunday afternoon when he and Madeline were the only two watching an Oregon Ducks football game. Per Michael, Madeline knew more about football than he did and almost cried when he got up to leave at halftime. In order not to hurt Madeline's feelings, my husband watched the entire game with her, politely nibbling on the green grapes and crackers she'd brought to share. He'd have much preferred watching the game at home while downing a few beers. To make up for lost time, he quickly guzzled two when he finally got back home.

As spring approached and the weather improved, folks in Spring Hill began to get out of their homes a bit more. Ninety-four-year-old Winifred took to sitting in her driveway in the afternoon sunshine, chatting with folks as they'd meander down to pick up their mail. One day I crossed the street to say hi.

"Have you heard from Eleanor?" I asked, knowing that Eleanor and Winifred had been friends.

"I'm giving her a chance to settle in before I call," Winifred said. "By the way, I really enjoyed reading your book."

"How'd you hear about my book?" I asked. I was surprised, since I had stopped telling people in this neighborhood that I was a writer.

"Eleanor told me about it and then loaned it to me." She paused and waved to another resident walking by. "You and I have a lot in common. My husband and I lived on a sailboat for twenty years, and then we RVed for several years before coming here."

I remembered a former writer friend, also in her nineties, in Florida who had lived with her husband on a sailboat for twenty years, just as Winifred had done. Like Winifred, this Florida friend had pointed out the similarities of living in an RV and on a boat. These two elderly women made me realize being a full-time RVer wasn't so special after all. Living on a boat was a far more exciting and less common way of living than in a recreational vehicle. Full-time RVers seemed to be a dime a dozen sometimes. My admiration for Winifred went up several more notches.

We chatted some more, primarily about Winifred's little lemon tree that she'd brought outside into the sunshine. The tree had one lemon that looked almost fully developed and multiple flowers, suggesting it was about to try to produce more fruit. I laughingly told Winifred she was "The Plant Whisperer" that she could coax a fruit tree to produce two distinct crops in the same season.

The driveway chat with Winifred roiled in my mind for a couple of days before my next course of action crystalized. The next time I saw her sitting outside, again beside her beloved lemon tree, I grabbed my second and third books, signed them, and took them to her.

"Oh, I'm so excited," she said. "Thank you. I'll start reading as soon as I go in this afternoon."

"Feel free to pass them along when you're done," I said.

"I might loan them out, but I'm certainly not going to give them away. I'm keeping them. I've never met anyone before who's written books."

After Winifred had had my books for several days, I found myself wondering several times a day whether she'd started reading them yet. As an accidental author with no formal training in writing, a low-grade insecurity, maybe even strong enough to call anxiety, had been with me nonstop since the release of my first book. Landing a publisher and watching my first book find gravity transformed me into a driven, somewhat psycho woman. I sometimes thought I'd completed a second and then a third book out of fear that my inadequacies and incompetencies would catch me if I didn't outrun them. Somehow, if I could keep writing and producing fast enough, no one would have time to realize my books were possibly inane and uninspired.

There's a term that's used when a writer feels like a fraud. It's called 'Imposter Syndrome.' Maya Angelou once said:

"Each time I write a book, every time I face that yellow pad, the challenge is so great. I have written eleven books, but each time I think, 'Uh oh, they're going to find out now. I've run a game on everybody and they're going to find me out."

Is there any other artistic endeavor with stakes that feel this high? I've met other writers who share this nagging, persistent feeling of being a fake. An imposter. Unlike musicians, a writer cannot make a sudden about-face to tweak or fine-tune a chord that didn't quite work, or a painter who can cover up strokes he didn't like by adding an additional layer. A printed word lasts forever, and once it's released into the world, there's no turning back.

Eleanor and my early observations in Spring Hill Park triggered a new understanding of myself as a writer. The lack of acknowledgment of my books from my neighbors stopped bothering me. If I wrote another book, it wouldn't be as an accidental author throwing a temper tantrum but rather as a focused old woman wrestling with the inevitability of decline and ultimately of death. Whatever the quality of work that I ultimately might produce, the completion of a book-length manuscript is an accomplishment most folks never achieve, even though many, many people make the remark, "Oh, I'm going to write a book one day. I just haven't gotten around to it yet." Of course, most people would have enough sense to never try to write a book, which I also understand and respect.

Maybe only masochistic folks ever sit down at a laptop with such a grueling and punishing goal as completing a 75,000+ word manuscript. There's a quote, sometimes attributed to Ernest Hemingway although scholars question the authorship, which goes like this: "There is nothing to writing. All you do is sit down at a typewriter and bleed." And that is about as good an example of masochism as I've ever heard.

I have many lessons to learn in my over-55 community. If I never write again, that'll be okay, too. But for today, perhaps it's enough to know that Eleanor and Winifred read and enjoyed my books.

That said, do I dare suggest to Winifred that she share my books with ninety-seven-year-old Madeline? I think I will. While I might be slowing down, here in Spring Hill I'm still living in the fast lane, and I welcome every new fan I can find.

As I meet more of my neighbors and get a broader sense of who lives here, I think I better understand why no one is impressed with my books. Many of the folks living in Spring Hill have advanced degrees and enjoyed long, successful careers prior to their retirement. Writing silly books about RV travel does not impress former college deans or folks who have published multiple mathematics, engineering, and finance books. Just as writing books doesn't impress local musicians, who think of performance art as the quintessential, highest form of creativity. I'm finding that elderly people are just as hard to impress as everyone else.

I appreciate the glimpse Eleanor gave me into aging. And speaking of temper tantrums, I could throw a major one over the complete and total lack of control anyone has over the journey and how we take our final walk. I don't want to be an Eleanor, with my last few years in a fearful, confused state with next door neighbors on both sides worried sick about me. Let me be a Winifred, sitting in the sunshine in the driveway, talking with the young whippersnappers in this over-55 neighborhood, and admiring my little lemon tree.

CHAPTER 11

Looking for Love

In our Spring Hill community, the single-woman households outnumbered the ones with couples at least five to one. My casual observations and conversations, both in the neighborhood and with every single woman I knew, left me convinced that most women in my age bracket were not looking for intimate relationships or another husband. They seemed contented with their lives, which they've filled with exercise, book clubs, gardening, music and art classes, other hobbies and interests, and lunches with other women. Most of the woman I've met within the past decade appeared happy flying solo.

As we began to make friends in Eugene, we found it interesting that we made more single friends of both men and women than we did couples. Maybe Eugene happened to be a place that embraced singles in the same way it embraced everything else. Most of the women we met fit the profile of our new neighborhood—content with their single status and not in the market for a partner.

Our friend Jeremy, my deceased friend Norma Jean's widower, came to visit us in the early summer of 2023, just six months after Norma Jean had passed away. This visit triggered some of the most interesting, poignant, and convoluted dating attempts imaginable, and Michael and I found ourselves with front row seats. We heard the stories and became immersed in the romance efforts of Jeremy and two other older men, all three on missions to find partners.

We knew Jeremy the best of the three single men and were privy to many more of his dating efforts. We were surprised to learn that shortly after Norma Jean passed away, he joined several online dating services, determined to find a replacement for the wife he'd so dearly loved.

Jeremy's focused discipline, strategic calculations, and unwavering confidence in his ultimate success in finding a mate should not have surprised me. He told us that on her deathbed, Norma Jean had made him promise to remarry. "She had a wife picked out for me already," he said. "It was one of our neighbors, and while the woman was really nice, she was just too old for me."

"How old was she?" I asked.

"Somewhere around sixty-four or sixty-five, I'd guess. I'm just not interested in women that old though. I find women in their late thirties or early forties much more interesting."

I struggled not to let my surprise show. Jeremy was sixty-eight years old. His deceased wife, whom he professed to have adored, had been older than he was by at least a couple of years. Why was he now focusing on younger women?

"It's just so much more work living alone," Jeremy said at another point. "Norma Jean and I had a system. She'd take care of everything inside and I'd take care of the outside. I'd really like to find someone to live with again."

My first thought was something to the effect: Is finding a new wife all about making life easier? Maintaining a household is work, no matter how many hands are pitching in. My second thought was shame that I could be so harsh. Hey, I told myself. Jeremy is where he is, and he's entitled to grieve and move on at his own pace.

"I've joined several online dating sites," he told us. "I can't believe how many women are responding to my profile." He paused, then added, "Hits from all over the world, and mostly from thirty- to forty-year-olds."

"I'd be careful if I was you," Michael said. "They could well be after your money."

"Oh, I know about that, and I won't let it happen. I've already had about two dozen women try to scam me. When I make it clear I'm not sending money, most of them never answer back."

"Would you really be interested in a woman that young?" I asked. "You're sixty-eight, right?"

"Yeah, but I don't have anything in common with women my age. I'm still active, interested in life, and ready to go places and do things."

Talk about feeling a bit stunned. Did he really say that to me? He must have forgotten that I am seventy-five years old, seven years older than he is. Where the hell is he coming from? This failure on my part to understand, in retrospect, was entirely my fault, not Jeremy's. I didn't have a clue at the time how loss could blind a person so profoundly.

If I'd given Jeremy's online dating quest more thought, I'd have also immediately understood his speed-mourning approach, his 'get 'er done and move on' attitude. He was a high-achieving, serious man who approached everything in life with discipline and focus. Naturally, he'd follow that familiar mode of operation to find a new spouse.

"I don't understand dating these days. It's been twenty-eight years since I've done this and I don't know what the expectations are," Jeremy told us with a shrug. "I've hired a dating coach to help me navigate this singles scene."

I sensed that Jeremy's announcement stunned Michael as much as it did me. "Huh?" was the most intelligible response I could muster. "Where did you find a dating coach?"

"I'd posted some questions on one of the dating sites, mainly about my confusion over today's expectations, and this guy in Toronto reached out to me on Facebook."

A million and one red flags exploded, with a warning light so intense it felt like it would blister my skin.

Michael recovered faster than I did. "That's interesting. How's that working out?"

"Good," Jeremy said. "It's really nice to have someone to talk with about how confusing this whole dating scene is."

"What are this guy's credentials?" I hated myself for asking but did it anyway. I'd gone the traditional, professional route—academic credentials, respected degrees, and appropriate licensing. My training had emphasized the protection of the public from untrained predators who made money off other people's problems.

"I don't know. He didn't tell me, and I didn't ask."

"Jeremy, I hate to say this, but as a social worker, I cringe when I hear about folks who hang out shingles and purport to help people with their problems. In Florida, I kept running into these folks who called themselves 'Life Coaches.' No credentials, no licensing, no oversight from the State, nothing but their own conviction that they had answers for other people's problems." I hated my agitation, the spittle that flew from my mouth, the jerks in my hands and arms as I waved and flapped. The idea of a dating coach had hit a sensitive nerve.

"I trust this guy," Jeremy said. "Don't' worry—no one's going to take advantage of me. I had three Zoom sessions with him before I signed the three-month contract. He's given me my money's worth already."

Shut the hell up, I told myself. This is not your business.

The conversation continued, and I listened as Michael effectively gave Jeremy his blessing on the dating coach who'd trolled him on an online dating site and charmed him into paying God-only-knows how much money for three months of coaching on how to navigate the singles scene.

"One thing I worry about with these younger women, though, is that they might want to have children," Jeremy said during another conversation. "My kids are grown, and I don't want to start another family." He shook his head with a sigh.

I couldn't help thinking his deceased wife, who'd been my close friend, would roll over in her grave if she'd heard this conversation. I wanted to tell him how the joke most likely was going to be on him if he ended up with a partner thirty years younger than he was. Never had biting my tongue felt so good, and in retrospect, I felt very proud for keeping my snarky and unwarranted opinions to myself.

I paid little attention as Jeremy and Michael continued to talk. Guy talk, as if I wasn't there. Talking about "things"—the kinds of things my women friends and I wouldn't typically discuss, such as climate change, politics, experiences in previous work situations. In my circles, women talked about personal things in their lives, including their feelings and reactions to things that happened.

Michael and I had had many "discussions" through our decades together when I'd wanted to talk through a situation or upcoming decision. A lot of these talks ended badly. Michael would invariably begin offering his opinion of what I should do, sometimes even using words like "should" and "don't." I'd respond by telling him I didn't need someone to tell me what to do, that I simply wanted him to listen because I was perfectly capable of making my own decisions. The conversation often ended with me feeling misunderstood and frustrated over our lack of communication.

As I listened to Michael "advise" Jeremy on how to find a new partner, and as I watched Jeremy hang on to every word and nod vigorously in agreement, I wondered if his new dating coach in Toronto had the same 'put out the fire and solve the problem' style of communicating as my husband's.

The amount of time Jeremy spent texting, emailing, and Facebooking while we hung out together increased. Exponentially. Finally, he explained. "I've hooked up with a couple of women from one of my online sites, and they're here in Springfield." He pulled out his phone, took a couple of seconds to pull up some info, and handed the phone to me. "That's one of the women who responded, and we've texted back and forth a few times." I looked at a couple of photos of an attractive woman with short, curly dark hair. "She's forty-eight and runs her own consulting business out of her home."

Michael reached for the phone. "Well, there you go. Are you going to meet her?"

"We're talking about it. I suggested we maybe meet at Sweet Cheeks Vineyards, the place where you guys took me yesterday. She said that would be okay, but that wine gave her headaches. She suggested we meet for a cup of coffee. Not sure what I think about that." Jeremy paused and a grimaced. "One of the problems Norma Jean and I had was that I enjoyed drinking and she didn't. I mean, it wasn't really a problem. She never said anything and was happy to sit with me in a bar or restaurant while I had a couple of drinks, but I always wished it was something she enjoyed doing, something we could share."

"Maybe this woman likes cocktails or beer," Michael said. "But if she's a nondrinker, I'd be wary that this'd be a good match for you."

Oh, Jeremy, I thought. How much muddling and bungling is in your future? Just the previous night, the three of us had gone to a concert and then met up with a couple of women friends afterwards. While our friend Maggie was an attractive, bright, competent woman, Jeremy didn't seem particularly interested. Maggie is sixty-nine, a year older than he is, but I knew she could more than give him a run for the money. Instead, Jeremy seemed enchanted with Shelley, a fifty-something dynamo wearing a short dress with a plunging neckline. Much to the surprise of both Michael and me, Shelley latched right on to Jeremy.

Jeremy and Shelley became Facebook Friends, and their Facebook interactions increased exponentially within the next few days, especially after he posted photos of his huge pickup truck and 35-ft. fifth wheel. Jeremy and his wife Norma Jean had started RVing following retirement, usually going south during the cold Colorado winters. It dawned on me that for a woman who'd been stuck in Eugene, or any other smallish city, the thought of chucking it all and riding off into the sunset in an RV might be a thrilling fantasy. (There was a time when I had had such fantasies, though mine were of taking off with a tall dark stranger on a Harley. This was after seeing *Easy Rider*.)

After meeting Shelley, I noticed a change in the way Jeremy dressed when we went out. He'd added a Fedora to his attire and had switched from plaid shirts to black t-shirts.

Jeremy was interested in everyone we knew and started sending Friend invitations to many of our Facebook Friends. Interacting with all these new Friends, many of whom were our friends, took a chunk of Jeremy's time, perhaps doubling the time he was already spending with his online dating sites. We teased him that he was starting to look like a teenager with his cellphone.

On the one hand, it was nice to see Jeremy's enthusiastic zest for life and optimism for the future. At the same time, I felt uneasy. I worried that this love quest was not going to work out well for him. I wanted to distance myself lest I inadvertently encourage him in decisions that might lead to his doom. Despite being a bright and competent man, Jeremy seemed startlingly naïve and trusting when it came to romance.

CHAPTER 12

Should Old People Plant Blueberries?

When Michael and I realized it was time to establish a homebase with a platoon of medical specialists, my number one criterion for a house was that it had a yard so I could garden again. In this respect, Spring Hill exceeded my expectations. I'd never realized that old people could get so excited and involved with their backyard gardens until I started meeting my new neighbors.

Gardening initially proved an instant conversation starter and way of getting to know people. It seemed that in almost every backyard in this neighborhood, owners had planted something edible. I'd not seen this in my neighborhood in Florida, where most folks stuck with ornamentals, perhaps because vegetables were so tough to grow due to high humidity, nematodes, year-round insects, and nutrient-poor sandy soil.

I felt like I'd landed slap-dab in the center of the Urban Homesteading movement. My new neighbors grew all kinds of fruits and vegetables in their backyards, and they offered me unending advice since I was a new Oregonian gardener.

Blueberries are my favorite fruit, and after learning that the Willamette Valley of Central Oregon was a primo growing environment for them, I decided I wanted to grow them in my backyard. The Oregon State University Extension Service website promised a harvest of "pounds of delicious fruit all season long." I'd already heard stories of two, three, sometimes even more blueberry bushes thriving in backyard gardens in our new neighborhood. My heart raced and my breath quickened.

My friend Polly, two houses down, had discovered several large blueberry bushes in her backyard when she moved into the neighborhood just a few months before Michael and I did. Unfortunately, we were not as lucky as Polly in the backyard gardening lottery, for our backyard was bereft of everything except grass, Rhododendrons, and Arborvitae, none of which I liked. Polly's backyard also included a fig tree, and she had shared huge, luscious figs with me in October when they ripened. I was so jealous of Polly's fig tree and vowed to try to maintain the friendship for the fig supply if nothing else.

In contrast to figs, my craving for blueberries was such that I would never rely on Polly's goodwill to share blueberries with me in the summer. My appetite for blueberries bordered on obsession, and I needed to take care of my own fix.

During a visit to the garden section at Jerry's Home Improvement Store in mid-April, I saw gorgeous, lush, two-foot-tall blueberry bushes. According to the tags, Monrovia, a premier hybridizer and grower of plants with national distribution, had grown these beauties. Polly had told me Monrovia had a huge nursery in Dayton, Oregon, a mere eighty miles up the road from Eugene. My mind raced. Locally grown, these blueberries would undoubtedly thrive in my backyard. And the bushes had so many flower buds I felt certain I'd be giving away blueberries by the bag-full, in addition to the bushels Michael and I would stuff into our own bottomless tummies.

The thought of walking out into my backyard and eating berries off the vine almost made me drool. Standing in that gardening aisle at Jerry's, it took tremendous self-discipline not to grab as many blueberry bushes as I could fit into my car and bring them home. Luckily, I controlled myself and wisely opted to learn more about blueberry cultivation before digging my Visa card out of my purse and holes in my backyard.

I began my online blueberry research with the Oregon State University Extension Service and quickly scanned the information. Initially, I liked what I learned. Insect and disease management, annual pruning, and feeding and watering all seemed manageable. I continued my online search, this time zeroing in on the nitty-gritty of blueberry horticulture.

My delicious dreams of blueberry cobblers, blueberry muffins, and blueberries by the fistfuls dissolved within the first five minutes of planting instructions. The Extension Service said I should take those lovely two-foot-tall, laden-with-flowers-and-buds Monrovia-grown bushes from Jerry's Home Improvement Center and prune them down to about four or five canes, making sure to remove every single bud. A bumper crop of blueberries during the first growing season in my backyard would turn any long-term dreams of bountiful future crops into a dismal disappointment, per the Extension Service's research-based information.

The explanation for this severe pruning made sense. During its first year in the ground, the plant needed to become established by spending its energy growing roots and shoots. Allowing the bush to produce fruit during its first year drained the plant's resources and dramatically reduced foliage and root growth. The plant would be subsequently weakened for life.

In the event I doubted what the Extension Service reported, the article included photos of two near-identical blueberry bushes planted side by side on the same day. Researchers had allowed the plant on the left to keep all those lovely flower buds and produce a bumper crop of luscious blueberries during its first season in the ground. They had severely pruned the plant on the right at the time of planting. When they pulled both plants from the ground two years later and photographed them, the fruit-producing bush was about a third the size of the heavily-pruned bush in both root-spread and the number of above-the-ground canes and leaves.

The Extension Service further reported that sometimes it takes a couple of years for a bush to produce any fruit at all and that it takes at least seven years for a bush to reach maturity. Given that the lifespan of a blueberry bush is about fifty years, I easily understood why it would behoove a grower to delay the immediate gratification of first-season production in favor of better long-term production, in every possible scenario except one. . . .

What if the planter of said blueberry bushes could not be guaranteed another seven years of life? And even if she did live seven more years, what if she was unwilling to accept less-than-optimal production until her plants reached maturity and gave her their best?

The planter to which I referred, of course, was myself. If I planted blueberry bushes in my backyard garden, I wanted to grab huge, juicy, delicious blueberries by the handfuls directly from my plants in the warm afternoon sun and stuff them into my mouth. I wanted to savor the taste, the smell, the sound of the pop as my teeth burst each berry's skin and its juice flooded my taste buds and dripped down my chin. Most importantly, I wanted all those pleasures next summer, not several years down the road, for I knew such sensations would produce happiness bordering on euphoria. When it came to blueberries, I did not value delayed gratification. I was already seventy-four years old and wasn't making any bets on my future.

It stunned me to realize I might be too old to plant blueberry bushes. My mind flashed to myriad other dreams that'd probably never materialize in the short time I had left to live. I'd never live abroad, I'd never earn a Ph.D., I'd never go into the Peace Corps, and I'd never again have the lush, tropical yard that had been my passion and pride and joy while living in Florida. My angst had nothing to do with blueberries. It was about my impending mortality.

Sometimes, when the weather is warm and sunny, ninety-four-year-old Winifred from across the street sits in her driveway with her straggly but beloved lemon tree, and I'll go over and chat with her a bit. Armed now with all my newfound knowledge about how to coax the best out of fruit-bearing plants, I wanted to tell Winifred she should certainly pluck the one large lemon growing on her tree and that she should probably strip every little flower and bud and not let the tree produce a single lemon for the next couple of years. But I hesitated to offer advice to this nonagenarian. She's had decades more Oregon gardening experience than I, and besides which, I got the feeling she was laughing at us all as well as at herself when she talked about her lemon tree.

During my last driveway chat with Winifred, I shared my blueberry dilemma about wanting to plant blueberries but being unsure whether

I had enough years left to do so. Her response suggested she was as wise about life as she was about gardening.

"I want to tell you a story," she said. "When my mother was in her mid-seventies, about your age, she decided she didn't like the afternoon sun shining in her bedroom, so she planted a tree outside her window for shade." Winifred paused and looked me in the eye. "Everybody laughed at my mother, saying she'd never live long enough for that tree to shade her window. But my mother was right. She lived another twenty years, and when she passed away, it was in the afternoon, lying on her bed and looking out her window at that 30-ft. tree, which now shaded her window."

Winifred was silent when she finished her story. It took me a minute to form my response.

"That's an inspiring story," I finally said. "It reminds me of that old saying about planting a tree being a belief in the future. Polly was certainly excited when she found blueberry bushes in her backyard. Maybe I should plant blueberries with the idea of making the next owners of my house happy, huh?"

Winifred smiled.

"Or maybe plant them with confidence that I'll enjoy picking and eating my own blueberries for many years," I added.

"There you go," my wise friend said.

With a new resolve, I left Winifred's driveway, determined to follow through on the pursuit of my blueberry dreams. I now believed I could prune a gorgeous Monrovia bush down to the nub and focus on long term rather than immediate rewards. For the next couple of years, I'd just make trips to nearby blueberry farms or to the nearby WinCo grocery store to satisfy my blueberry appetite.

I tackled the Extension Service website again and began taking extensive notes. I realized in short order that I was far from being ready to bring one or more of those vibrant blueberry bushes home from Jerry's, even after deciding I could do the necessary pruning and forfeiting of berries the first year.

Location, soil, and pH seemed to be the most important initial factors. I studied my backyard, tracing the sun's path, trying to anticipate how its trajectory would change as the days lengthened and the angles changed. My blueberries would need at least six full hours of sun daily, preferably more. Due to neighbors' trees and my fence, location was a bit tricky, made more difficult because I really didn't want to dig up the grass in the middle of the yard. The fencerows were clear already and bereft of much foliage. In time, I decided my southern fencerow would work. Plants there would receive both morning and afternoon sun, minus a few hours in midday from what my neighbor's rapidly growing Red Maple tree might block.

The next hurdle proved a bit more vexing. It seems that blueberries are particular about soil, especially little things like drainage and pH. For drainage, the Extension Service said blueberries needed "well-drained sandy loam or clay loam with moderate water-holding capacity." As I walked along the fencerow where my blueberries would grow, my shoes squished in the rain-saturated soil. This water retention felt like a notch or two above "moderate," and I guessed that blueberries wouldn't like wet feet any more than I did as I felt water oozing into my shoes. (The Spring Hill community sat on land that was once a part of a riverbed. Contractors had hauled in tons of fill dirt prior to the construction of homes. However, underground rivers continued to exist, and many of the homes in the area, ours included, needed sump pumps in their basements to pump out seeping water on an ongoing basis.)

This little drainage issue along my fencerow seemed minor compared to the stuff I read about soil preparation. The Extension Service recommended I take soil samples for testing a year or more before I planned to plant my blueberries. A link on the website gave specific instructions for how to take this sample, how many samples I'd need, how much the testing would cost, and where I should drop off my samples. The lab results would give me readings on six important variables: pH, Potassium, Calcium, Magnesium, Boron, and Organic Matter. The soil sample report would include ideal ranges for all these needed blueberry nutrients and what I should do to make my soil adequate.

The process of adjusting my soil readings to pass blueberry muster could take up to a year. I'd need to add amendments, wait a few months and re-test, make more adjustments as needed, and continue to add and test until all readings fell within the recommended parameters. I felt weary just thinking about all the time, energy, and expense of digging and mixing all those supplements in with my native soil. During all those months of tinkering, my fencerow would lay fallow, producing only weeds.

My excitement about a blueberry patch in my backyard withered a bit more when I re-visited the math. I again took note of my age, seventy-five by this time, for this was a full year after we'd moved into Spring Hill. If I returned to Jerry's right this moment and snatched up several of those Monrovia blueberry bushes and planted them tomorrow, taking my chances on drainage, pH, and soil quality, and if I did the recommended initial severe pruning, I'd probably be seventy-seven or seventy-eight before I plucked the first delicious, sun-warmed blueberry from a bush in my backyard. Even more depressing, I'd be eighty-two before my bushes reached maturity and gave me their all. My heart began to break.

This morning, as I scanned my daily email, I noticed a new online seminar scheduled for a fall release on "Picky Fruit: Establishing Blueberries in a Home Garden." Given my current preoccupation and disappointment with all that I'd recently learned about the possibility of a lovely blueberry patch in my backyard, I sighed at the irony. I'd initially believed my little backyard in Eugene would be the perfect setting for several blueberry bushes. Disheartened at all that I'd read, I could only laugh that now even the Extension Service used the term "picky" to describe these damnable berries. What had happened to that earlier promise that the Willamette Valley was a blueberry grower's paradise?

I regrouped. The only sensible thing I could do at this time would be to take soil samples and drop them off at the Extension Service for testing. In six months when the Picky Fruit seminar took place, I'd hopefully be on my way to having the soil along my fencerow adjusted for those persnickety berries. I felt certain that by 2024, Monrovia would have come up with even better hybrids that I could scarf up from a local big box store.

Did it really matter if I'd be eighty-three when the results of my labor reached full fruition? Winifred's mother had believed in the future, and that faith rewarded her with lovely afternoon shade for her bedroom window because she'd planted a tree while in her mid-seventies.

In the meantime, however, I think there's room along that fencerow for a nice fig tree. I've read that figs are fast growers and not particularly finicky about soil. I believe I could learn to crave and relish figs with an enthusiasm approximating my blueberry obsession. And maybe, just maybe, my friend Polly down the street, who'd generously shared figs with me back in the fall, will graciously offer me a few bowlfuls of blueberries this summer. I can only hope.

Two years later, I congratulate myself on the wise decision not to plant blueberries along my Southern fencerow. At the same time, I kick myself for having planted a sun-loving fig tree there. The fig tree languished, even in this Pacific Northwest climate where gardeners celebrate the rapid growth and excellent production from their fruits and vegetables. I finally dug up the fig tree and gave it to my yard guy Manny, who was delighted and said he had a perfect place to plant it in his yard.

One would think, after all this interminable obsessing and ruminating, I'd figure out something appropriate to plant along my fencerow, right? So, what did I do? I planted another sun-loving fruit-producing plant—a Hardy Banana. I can hardly wait to see how many months it'll be in the ground before I dig it up and give it to Manny since it isn't getting enough sun.

I must wonder if maybe I'm not only too old to plant blueberries; I just might be too old to plant anything. Might my continued poor judgment in plant choices be a sign of early dementia? Or maybe I'm just burning out on the overwhelming project of taking a near-empty backyard and transforming it into the lush, mature, and charming garden of my dreams. Yes, this blueberry, fig, and banana triumvirate of bloopers makes me feel decidedly old. And perhaps a tad inept.

CHAPTER 13

Feeling Twelve Again

I hadn't realized how time-consuming daily living had been as full-time RVers. We had to plan routes, secure campground reservations, and attend to millions of other details. Because of the lack of storage space, we often shopped daily for groceries. When it came time to travel, which could be as often as every day, we had to unhook water, electricity, and sewage hoses, pack up grills and outside furniture, and hook up our tow car to the RV. We also had to secure many items inside the rig lest they fall, break, or spill on bumpy roads. When we'd arrive at our new campsite, we did all these chores in reverse.

Settling down in a house after living in a motorhome left me feeling a bit adrift. In our new over-55 digs, all our utility connections remained attached, our refrigerator and freezer held a month's supply of food, and our home base parking spot was always in our garage. I found myself in need of additional ways to fill my time, especially something that would get me outside in the fresh air and sunshine and provide a means of exercise. (In addition to gardening, which was always my preferred outside activity.)

Historically, Michael and I had hiked four or five times a week, but his mobility issues had progressed to the extent that I couldn't depend on that for exercise. In fairness, my poor arthritic feet hurt most of the time, and those long hikes we used to take were proving increasingly difficult for me, just as they were for Michael.

I decided to buy a bicycle, hoping I could solve the need for exercise as well as recapture the rush that I used to feel while riding. I wanted to feel twelve years old again, not the seventy-five I was. My childhood bicycle had introduced me to the freedom of being alone in the world, away from the supervision, control, and judgments of others. I needed to reclaim my independent spirit. Time was no longer on my side the way it used to be. I didn't have time to lollygag.

It had been six years since I'd last ridden. Michael and I had been avid cyclists, although neither our distances nor times would have impressed anyone other than the two of us. Our longest distance had been a whopping forty-five miles one Saturday morning. Exhausted but exhilarated, it took a couple of days for us to recover physically. We were spring chickens back then, in our mid-forties and still under the mistaken notion that our bodies would last forever.

Typical rides for us back then were about twenty miles, which we'd try to do five times a week. Florida was flat, which made pedaling easy and fast. We always celebrated our safe return home after a ride, since getting to the bike path required four miles out and back on a four-laned highway with a largely ignored 55-mph speed limit. I look back and cringe at our apparent obliviousness to the danger of riding on this busy road. I suppose our youth back then made us feel immune to injury and death.

A motorist knocked Michael off his bicycle one time on this major throughfare. We were riding single file in the bike lane and approaching an intersection where the traffic light was red. The intersection was congested as we zipped forward towards the light. Without warning, a driver in the far-right lane made a turn into a bank parking lot rather than turning at the light. She made her turn just in time to hit Michael as he pedaled by the entrance to the bank, sending him sprawling into the bank's driveway.

"Michael," I screamed as I rushed towards him, "are you okay?" Stupid question, I realized as soon as the words left my mouth. Despite bloody road rash on his knee and an elbow, a scraped palm, and a pinky bent at an unnatural angle, Michael managed to get himself up off the pavement, stagger towards the sidewalk, and plop down on the grass. I moved his damaged bike out of the driveway. The light changed at the intersection, but none of the motorists who'd witnessed the accident bothered to stop.

The woman who hit Michael at least had the courtesy to stop her car and step outside. Her first concern was not with Michael's injuries but rather with potential damage to her car. She inspected her right front fender before walking over to address her victim.

"My car is scratched and dented," she reported. "Want to give me your insurance info?"

"Aren't you concerned about whether he's hurt?" My outrage at this idiot's reaction was intense. "Michael, we need to call the sheriff's department and an ambulance."

"Why would you call the cops? You were the one who pulled out in front of me," she said. "You'll get a ticket."

"Huh? I don't think so," Michael said. His face reflected his amazement at her words. "I was in the bike lane, and you turned to the right and hit me dead center."

"Hey buddy," the now irate hysterical driver screamed. She pulled her skirt up to just above her knee and pointed to a scar. "See this? An abusive boyfriend did this to me, so I don't feel sorry for you."

It'd be a tossup as to whether Michael or I was more stunned. Neither of us said or did a thing as we watched the woman storm back to her car and peel out of the parking lot. Although positive he'd broken his finger when he went down, my stubborn husband refused to go to an emergency room, feeling that he could splint the finger himself as well as clean his raw knee, elbow, and palm of road grime. We were only a mile from home, so I hurried home on my bike and returned with the car to pick up Michael and his damaged bike. In time, Michael managed to find humor and turned the incident into a funny story.

Looking back, I'm surprised we didn't give up cycling after that accident. If a crazy distracted driver had nudged one of our bikes while driving sixty miles per hour down Ehrlich Road, it would probably have been an end game. But Michael and I never talked about that possibility. The idea of giving up riding because of safety concerns simply never occurred to us. The adrenaline rush of cruising along at fifteen miles per hour, the wind in our faces, the sun on our backs, and the near-rapturous rush from the physical exertion from our then strong, healthy bodies was not a feeling we'd voluntarily abandon.

Now that we lived in Eugene, I realized bicycling was the only exercise I'd ever found addicting and exhilarating. I had discovered through cycling the joy of athleticism, although rather late in the game in terms of my age. I was in my forties then.

In total, Michael and I rode bicycles for about a quarter of a century. When we decided to become RVers, we'd load the bicycles on the bike rack attached to the car, hook up the car to the motorhome, and off we'd go. Riding became a favorite way of checking out new places while traveling across the country and parts of Canada. It never occurred to us that this joy might one day end.

The end of our bicycling heydays came on Halloween Day in 2017 when Michael tripped on a cracked chunk of sidewalk while power walking in our Tampa neighborhood. He fell on his left shoulder, breaking the head of his humerus in four places. Surgery was unsuccessful and the injury never healed properly. The shoulder joint remained rigid and frozen. Second opinions from other surgeons did not recommend further intervention, since the same thing would likely happen again. Because of chronic pain, a subsequent sequelae of balance issues, and progressive reductions in range of motion of the arm and shoulder, Michael's bicycle riding days were over. To this day, Michael is unable to touch the top of his head with his left hand, although a Eugene surgeon is optimistic that another surgery could leave Michael with less pain and more mobility.

Selling our beautiful, well-loved hybrid Trek bicycles, accessories, and riding gear broke our hearts. I could have kept riding without Michael, but at this point in our retirement and RVing, we spent five or six months of the year traveling. I couldn't really see myself exploring unfamiliar areas without my riding buddy. I accepted the end with equanimity, feeling blessed to have enjoyed the sport for as long as I had. I would need to find other, equally satisfying ways of getting exercise, enjoying the outdoors, and finding respite from the chaotic and frenetic world. Unfortunately, I never found anything comparable to riding.

When I realized that Eugene was relatively flat, just as Florida had been, that the weather permitted riding almost year-round, and that the town had such a beautiful network of riding trails, I couldn't resist.

What a serendipity to further realize that in Eugene, I lived just a couple of miles from the northern trailhead for the Willamette River Trail System and only a half mile from the beginning of the I-5 Springfield Trail System. Both trail systems were specifically intended for hiking, bicycling, and other non-motorized recreation. (Although I did see and hear a fair number of e-bikes zipping past me at what I perceived as alarming speeds.) But, unlike Ehrlich Road and the route to the bike trail in Tampa, in Eugene the two-mile ride to the trail was along two lanes of traffic with a 35-mph speed limit, which motorists obeyed.

Bicycling in Eugene began to appear as safe as walking around the block. The aligned signs indicated this was what I needed to do. I could only hope that my advanced age, slower reflexes, and God-only-knows what other potential limitations would not prove my new Trek hybrid an unwise purchase.

In terms of possible motivations for that purchase of a bicycle by a seventy-five-year-old coot, now a resident in an over-55 community and approaching an emotional meltdown of the nth degree, I will defend that bicycle purchase to my death. I refused to succumb to cautious trepidations. While I feared a fall, broken bones, pulverization by a car (or better yet a bus or a semitruck), I would *not* deny myself the pleasure I wanted and needed today with the purchase of a bicycle. Could living in Spring Hill be making me spunkier? Or maybe just more stupid?

CHAPTER 14

Vehicles of Doom

As I stood at my kitchen counter one morning, reading the paper and eating breakfast, I glanced out the window and saw a firetruck pull up across the street. Oh, no, I thought, watching two firefighters descend from the cab. The guy from the passenger side opened a back basement door and removed his orange supply bag. I knew the sterile blue gloves would go on as soon as he entered the house and reached his patient. I'd seen this routine before with Eleanor.

A couple of minutes later, an ambulance arrived. Shortly after that, a supervisor in a red pickup pulled up behind the ambulance.

"Oh, no, Michael," I said. "Think someone died? Why would a supervisor be showing up on a 911 call?"

"Who knows? Maybe someone croaked, or maybe there's a new hire that the guy wants to observe on the job."

I'd met my neighbor Callie who lived cattycornered across the street from where these emergency vehicles had parked, but I didn't know her. Winifred lived next door to Callie, but the fire truck blocked the view of Winifred's house, so I couldn't tell which house the paramedics had entered.

I'd learned from Winifred that Callie's husband was a non-ambulatory shut-in with multiple health issues. Callie was his caregiver and hardly ever left his side. Even when she took long walks around the neighborhood every morning, she'd stop and check on him two or three times. Winifred further told me Callie always carried her cell phone and made sure her husband had his cell in his lap with her number punched in.

Callie's circumstances tumbled and roiled in my mind. I'd heard of other women in Spring Hill who spent almost their entire waking hours caring for spouses. Some had occasional relief in the form of paid personnel who came in for short periods of time, but for the most part, these women cared for their invalid men with little to no outside help.

Standing at my kitchen window, I wondered what it would be like to be totally responsible for a spouse's care. Would a situation like Callie's be in my future? Michael's declining health scared the bejesus out of me. Maybe learning about the kinds of situations others faced daily would help me prepare for the future. While I didn't know anyone with a crystal ball or psychic insight into the future, I nevertheless assumed that one day I'd be caring for Michael. I could only hope I'd rise to the occasion when that time came. Moving into Spring Hill with potential caregiving role models suddenly felt like one of our better decisions.

I realized, of course, as I worried and virtually rehearsed multiple end-game scenarios, a car could hit me on Crescent Avenue tomorrow as I blithely bicycled along, thinking I owned the world. Or a physician could diagnose me with an aggressive, fatal disease and give me three months to live. I had no more promise of tomorrow than anyone else in this damned little over-55 park, which they should have named the almost-85 community. I could be dead by next Wednesday.

After Eleanor moved out, there were fewer emergency vehicles on our street. Paramedics had hauled off the woman directly across the street from us in the yellow house on a gurney a few weeks earlier. I'd watched the paramedics bring her down her walkway and load her into the truck. During the process, she'd been sitting up and texting on her phone, so I'd correctly assumed she wasn't in any life-threatening situation. She was back home the next day. I'd walked across the street when we first moved in and introduced myself to her. She hardly said hello and had turned around and walked back inside her house. So much for friendliness, I'd thought, and promptly forgot her name. I later learned she was ninety-four years old, so maybe I should have been a bit more patient.

Whatever was going on now across the street did not seem to be an emergency. Firefighters and paramedics appeared to be moving in slow motion, but then, I'd never seen them move very quickly under any circumstances. They all just seemed eternally unflappable.

Finishing my breakfast and the Register Guard, I didn't want to leave my kitchen window lest I miss the outcome of what might be the only excitement of the day on my street. After Eleanor moved to independent living, I'd found myself sometimes missing the stimulation of big red trucks despite the fact they never flashed their red lights or turned on their sirens. I started unloading the dishwasher as a way of justifying my continued voyeurism, realizing as I did so that I sorely needed to get a life.

Why were they taking so long in that house? I desperately hoped the guy hadn't died, although I wouldn't have minded a husband/wife team across the street who might become our friends. Even after a year in this over-55 community, we'd only found one couple with enough common interests to form a basis for anything more than a casual friendship. I winced at how unkind and self-serving my thoughts were about my neighbors across the street. Some of my reactions about life in Spring Hill left me feeling bad about myself.

Thinking of my Spring Hill neighbor's possible demise, I remembered an emergency vehicle sighting from 2021 when Michael and I were hiding from Covid-19 in a remote RV resort in Desert Hot Springs, California. We had joined about forty members of our RV club for a winter retreat. We all sought safety, good weather, and social and recreational opportunities.

One evening, Michael and I surreptitiously watched a fire truck and an ambulance ease into the RV park, lights flashing but sirens muted, and stop at the motorhome next to ours. We'd briefly met the man who lived there, who had explained that his wife had serious health issues and never left their motorhome. The mysterious drama of watching four uni-formed first responders, two from each vehicle, go in and out of the rig lasted over an hour. They made multiple cell phone calls from the yard, exchanged places from inside to outside so that there were always two paramedics inside and two sitting or standing outside. They exchanged places in what looked like a paramedic changing of the guard.

Michael and I were able to watch all this from the comfort of our dining area inside our motorhome. By keeping our lights off, we were able to see everything going on next door without either our next-door neighbor or any of the first responders spotting us. I'd have been embar-rassed had anyone caught us engaged in such childish, sneaky spying.

"What kind of musical chairs are they playing over there?" Michael asked.

"Dunno, but it's like watching a slow-motion dance of uniforms. They're not acting like there's any emergency."

"I'm wondering if she died," Michael said. "Maybe they're waiting for law enforcement."

"Would they call law enforcement if there was no sign of foul play?"

"Who knows? Maybe they have a special kind of ambulance to trans-port dead bodies."

Although getting tired of sitting in the dark, Michael and I never-theless persevered. After almost two hours, a third emergency vehicle arrived, this one also an ambulance. Two additional paramedics got out with what again seemed to be no sense of urgency. Eventually, the two newly arrived paramedics removed a stretcher from their ambulance and took it into the RV. The fire truck and its two first responders pulled out and left the RV park.

Next came the part that freaked me out and left an indelible memory. After about ten minutes, the door opened. The two outside paramedics jumped to attention, and the two inside uniforms began turning the stretcher sideways to maneuver it around and through the narrow RV doorway and down the steep steps. Our neighbor's wife appeared to be inside a body bag strapped on the stretcher with wide belts. When the first responders finally got her down the steps, they loaded her into the newly arrived ambulance, again with no sense of the kind of emergency a firetruck, two ambulances, and six guys in uniforms would have suggested. After saying goodbyes to each other and to the husband, the four paramedics drove away in their two ambulances, with the woman strapped down in the back of one of them.

Fifteen minutes later, from our still-clandestine dinette observation spot, we saw the husband calmly leave his rig, get in his car, and drive off.

"Oh my God, Michael. She's dead, don't you think?"

"I don't know. This was all very confusing, but it did look like a body bag."

"We should let someone know, don't you think?"

"Yeah, I guess."

I got on the phone, calling our group host as well as our best friends next door. Word spread quickly. Within fifteen minutes, at least a third of our group (of about thirty-five RVers) had congregated in the street to speculate, reflect, and try to figure out what had happened and what we might do to help. Since Michael and I were the only ones in the group who knew the man, and since I had been the one to report the incident to our host, I agreed to keep the group updated as we gained more information.

Two days passed before we saw our neighbor again, and we rushed over the minute he reached his door. Luckily, I had the wherewithal not to start expressing condolences but rather to begin by asking what had happened.

We'd been correct about there being no emergency, but it wasn't because of a dead body. The guy told us his wife had fallen, something he said happened often, but that this time he hadn't been able to get her up. "She didn't seem to be hurt, but the paramedics thought she should be transported and kept overnight for observation anyway," he told us. "Plus, they didn't think it was safe for her to be here under these conditions, that maybe she ought to go to a rehab facility and get physical therapy, maybe build up her strength a bit."

While I've made embarrassing mistakes many times in my life, this one rattled me more than most. I couldn't believe I'd reported a death in our group when there hadn't been a death after all. I hightailed it down to our host's site, hoping I could spread the word that our neighbor was alive before anyone expressed condolences to the husband.

"But what the hell was that body bag about?" I couldn't let it go. I brought up the wife, the three emergency vehicles, and what we so clearly thought we had seen several times a day for at least a week. Not only to Michael, but to several of our neighbors as well. It haunted me, and I haunted both Michael and my neighbors with my nonstop verbal obsessing over my mortifying mistake. I cringed to think that the husband might somehow learn that I'd reported to our group that his wife had died.

Had there been anything other than Covid and vaccines to obsess about during January 2021, I don't think I would have ruminated over my misinterpretation of what happened next door. Although members of our group assured me the mistake would have been easy to make, I'm not sure anyone believed they'd be so stupid as to confuse live and dead bodies on a stretcher.

As a postscript to this story, about three days after his wife was admitted into the hospital, the husband told us there was an outbreak of Covid on the floor she was on. Our next-door neighbor could no longer visit, and he had no idea what this outbreak of the virus would mean.

Michael and I left Desert Hot Springs about a week later, the very day after getting our first coronavirus vaccines, so we have no idea how this story ultimately ended. I still think about it from time to time, especially after moving into Spring Hill and realizing how fragile and medically vulnerable some of our neighbors were.

🛺

Meanwhile, in my kitchen in Spring Hill, I grew restless trying to maintain a vigil of the slow-motion scene across the street. I saw a stretcher removed from the ambulance with no sense of urgency. A half hour later, I saw the firefighter return his orange supply bag to its storage place, and I watched as the two firefighters drove away. Next the ambulance and the fire department's pickup truck left. I panicked to realize I'd not seen the stretcher return to the ambulance.

I immediately texted my next-door neighbor Mary Lou. "Do you know what's going on?" I asked. I briefly described what I'd seen.

"No, and I'm not home. I'll check with Callie and let you know what I find out."

Jeez, I thought. Could they have wheeled a body out as I leaned down to grab clean silverware out of the dishwasher? How could I have missed that?

A little later, Mary Lou got back to me. "It wasn't Callie's husband they came for. It was Winifred. I'll let you know if I find out anything else."

Oh, no. Not ninety-four-year-old Winifred the Plant Whisperer who sang to her plants and sweet-talked her little lemon tree.

Bottom line, another emergency vehicle observational disaster had occurred, one almost as ridiculous as the one in Desert Hot Springs. This time, I'd been staking out the wrong house, and the ambulance had blocked my view of Winifred's driveway, meaning I'd not seen the stretcher leave Winifred's house and paramedics loading her into the ambulance.

"Michael," I finally said later that day, after having fretted and stewed for hours over my inept situational awareness, "I think I need to give up voyeurism and try to find something meaningful to do with my life."

"Good idea," he said.

Jerk, I thought.

A couple of days later Mary Lou told me Winifred was back home from the hospital, adding that she had no further details. She said she planned to call Winifred in a few days.

I wondered about the propriety of knocking on a ninety-four-year-old's front door to inquire about her health. I wanted to know how Winifred was right this minute, not in a few days. Yet, I'd heard this before in this neighborhood. There seemed to be no sense of urgency whatsoever about checking on and getting updates on people's health. While these neighbors might think they had all the time in the world to obtain information, I believed the clocks were ticking in overtime for every one of us.

But maybe, if I reached my eighties or nineties, I, too, would accept a more leisurely approach to community updates. I guessed my spring chicken impatience must look like impulsive immaturity to these older residents of Spring Hill. And maybe if I really live to be that old, my fascination with all these emergency vehicles and uniformed first responders will have dwindled.

One thing I knew for certain: I didn't want to ever look out my kitchen window and see those emergency vehicles in front of my house. They must never, ever come for me or Michael, not until I was better prepared than I was today.

CHAPTER 15

Who'd Want an Old Man?

I found myself concerned about Jeremy's single-minded quest for a woman. His now deceased wife had been my good friend. On one level, it seemed disloyal and disrespectful that he seemed to have moved on so quickly after her death. Had he not loved her? Had he spent his twenty-eight years with her fantasizing about drop-dead gorgeous forty-year-olds? He seemed to prioritize looks and age over intelligence, personality, values, and other traits. The characteristics he said were important to him, in my opinion, hinted at an objectification of women, and that attitude riled my feminist sensibilities. How dare he? I hated it when men looked at women like that.

Mixed in with my anger over Jeremy's chauvinism was concern for his well-being. He seemed incredibly naïve and trusting, seeming to take at face value any cockamamie story, no matter how bizarre, every potential dating partner gave him. Unless Jeremy was presenting himself as wealthy, which we doubted he would do, I couldn't understand why thirty-eight and forty-year-olds would give him the time of day. He acted so eager to find a mate that he seemed oblivious to the potential long-term heartache a woman thirty or so years his junior could bring.

I was happy that Michael had a similar interpretation of Jeremy's behavior and shared my concerns. "He's going to get scammed out of every penny to his name," Michael said. "He doesn't even see it coming, but some pretty little thing is going to take him to the cleaners, and he'll never know what hit him."

I agreed completely, but I didn't understand how Michael could have had those fears for Jeremy's future and not be concerned about his sixty-seven-year-old friend Bill, who recently hooked up with a twenty-eight-year-old babe from Thailand. Bill frequently posted photos on Facebook of this girlfriend. Usually, the photos had been taken on Bill's boat, and the girlfriend most often wore only a bikini and a smile. Michael showed me some of the pics, pointing out that Bill's smile was bigger than the girlfriend's. I mulled this over, trying to zero in on what bothered me most about that scene.

I didn't think I was jealous, not of that Thai woman's youth nor of her beauty. I wasn't bad-looking at her age, and I wouldn't want to be a clueless twenty-eight-year-old again. I didn't think I was particularly bothered that my husband found that young woman's body worthy of intense scrutiny. Probably at some level, and maybe it wasn't even very deep, Michael would have loved to have found himself in his friend's shoes, even if just for a day. If my husband left me to pursue a beautiful young woman, I might laugh, knowing that ultimately the outcome would probably prove disappointing for both Michael and the young woman. If he left me for a younger woman, I might even feel relief to have only my own aging issues to contend with and wouldn't have to worry about his, too.

I thought some more about how women my own age reacted to Jeremy's attempts to find a partner. I couldn't call Jeremy a womanizer, since he'd had virtually no luck in even snagging a date from all those dating sites. It was just as well, I realized, that Jeremy wasn't interested in the sixty- and seventy-year-olds since the ones I knew probably wouldn't have been interested in him anyway.

An epiphany arose. Perhaps Jeremy, Michael's friend Bill, and all the other gray-haired, paunch-bellied older men who focused on younger women had a greater chance of success with these young targets than they would have had with women their own ages.

Remembering my Florida writer friend who'd lived on a sailboat with her husband for twenty years, I eventually had asked her how she felt when her husband died and she had to make a new life for herself on land. "It was fine," she said. "I'd spent all those years on that boat, but now the future was mine. It was finally my time." She put a strong emphasis on the word "my."

My friend's words resonated. When I think of how my conversations with women friends have changed through the years, I realize that with each passing year, the women I know seem to become less and less interested in establishing relationships with men. I don't know a single woman over fifty who'd want to remarry if something happened to her partner.

Meanwhile, I suppose I need to get off Jeremy's case about his interest in younger women and be his friend, regardless of his choices. He was a loyal, devoted, and excellent partner for my dead friend, and he'll make a good partner for the next woman, regardless of how old or young she is. I think the greatest heartache ahead for Jeremy is when he realizes he's not going to ever find anyone as perfect for him as my friend Norma Jean had been.

As for Michael, I watch with interest as he eagerly asks Jeremy for daily updates on his online dating progress. I try to read my husband's reactions, wanting to know if and how his reactions might change over time as we follow Jeremy's life into the future. I hope Michael is also paying a lot of attention to Bill and his Thai girlfriend.

As I watch Jeremy's attempts to deal with the loss of his wife, I vow not to make the same mistake Norma Jean did. On my deathbed, should Michael be the surviving spouse, I would never make him promise to remarry. I'd beg him to develop as many friends as possible, to find comfort wherever and however he could, and to do everything possible to live a rich, full, and happy life. That "M" word feels too much like a landmine for me to even mention. Plus, I'd hate to think only six months after my death I might be rolling over in my grave at what my widowed husband was up to.

My big question, after obsessing about these issues and questions for over a year now, is what are old men to do? Does anyone really want an old man for who or what he is? The younger women are most likely looking for sugar daddies who'll take care of them financially, maybe emotionally as well. The older retired and widowed women are likely tired of taking care of men and appreciate the freedom of being single again, after they've recovered from their grief if they've lost a spouse.

Such speculations trigger yet another jolting realization. Quite possible, no one really wants old women either. Jeremy and Bill are probably the rule, not the exception, in wanting attractive, spry younger women who'll make them feel young and vibrant again. The question is not really who wants an older man but rather who wants an older person, period. I suppose I'd find it devastating if I were to suddenly become a widow, realize I wanted male companionship, and not be able to find a man who found me interesting and attractive.

Perhaps the truth I've avoided admitting throughout a year and a half of watching Jeremy struggle unsuccessfully to find a partner is that . . . maybe no one finds older people of either sex attractive. Or maybe it takes a truly exceptional person to get beyond physical appearances and appreciate qualities such as kindness, compassion, and intelligence.

As my at-times wise husband always says, "The assholes are equally distributed between the sexes."

Rather than focusing on Jeremy and all the 'mistakes' I believe he's making, I might better invest my energies on trying to become the best possible person ever so I'd look attractive to a partner in the future, just in case I outlived Michael and longed for a man.

CHAPTER 16
Manny the Gardener

How did I become so emotionally reactive toward the dude who comes twice a month to cut the grass, edge the flowerbeds, and tidy up the Candyland-sculptured shrubs in my yard? His name is Manny, and I hired him for yard maintenance shortly after we moved into our house.

All the homes in Spring Hill have small front yards and larger back yards. At least half a dozen gardening crews descended daily into the neighborhood, some with trucks bearing the names of landscape companies and others in owner-owned trucks with no signage or logos. Most of these trucks towed trailers loaded with industrial-sized mowers, edgers, blowers, chain saws, and other landscape tools. I can attest to the ridiculous noise level these huge gas-powered machines emit in this neighborhood every weekday and sometimes even the weekends.

Competition is fierce among these crews to sign up the new residents. Men from two different yard services accosted Michael and me the day we started moving in. We held out, wanting more information before committing.

Manny came recommended to me by next-door neighbor Mary Lou. I later learned that Mary Lou paid a Master Gardener to come monthly to examine her plants and make suggestions for additions, removals, and interventions. I found this information rather curious. I knew the guidelines of the Master Gardener program, which was an international volunteer organization with bylaws. One of its rules prohibited volunteers from accepting money for their services, so that tidbit from Mary Lou piqued the question in my mind of whether Lane County, Oregon, might have a rogue in their program. But I forgot about the Master Gardeners when Mary Lou took me on a tour of her backyard and pointed out the raised gardening beds with drip irrigation systems that Manny had built for her. My heart went pitter-pat, and I knew I'd found my man. "You'll be pleased with Manny," Mary Lou assured me.

I began to sense that gardening competition in this neighborhood extended far beyond the maintenance crews who did most of the actual work. I later pieced together that Mary Lou's Master Gardener was for designing, planting, and troubleshooting problems. Lawn care, including fertilization and pest control, was Manny's domain.

Many of the older residents in the neighborhood were physically unable to keep up their yards, especially to the high standards to which this community aspired. I could probably count on my fingers the number of homeowners who mowed their own grass or edged their own sidewalks. While I felt that I could probably still physically mow, edge, and trim, I didn't want to invest in the equipment. Plus, I wanted to spend my gardening energies planting and creating something beautiful, not managing backdrops and fillers. My new neighbors assured me the Willamette Valley was God's Country when it came to gardening and that I'd be amazed at how quickly my new plants would grow.

The Spring Hill Park manager informed us during our application process that he conducted routine inspections of the grounds and issued citations to homeowners whose front yards didn't comply with community standards. The manager assured me, however, that he didn't care what anyone did in their backyards. That knowledge pleased me, since garden funk was my former specialty. I loved combing thrift stores, garage sales, and curbsides on trash pick-up days to find unique garden art. I had filled my Florida backyard with mirrors hung on fences, container gardens nestled into huge hedgerows, and even a life-sized, fiberglass Black Angus beef steer to remind me of my farm-girl roots.

My ambivalence about Manny started early on. Unlike the other maintenance crews in the community where many of the guys worked for larger companies, Manny was self-employed. Also, his yard crew partner was his wife Carmen, the only female lawn "guy" in the neighborhood. I initially thought this was rather cool but soon began to wonder about the distribution of power in their teamwork.

This was my first experience with a lawn service. In my previous houses, I'd taken pride in doing everything myself. I didn't want Michael messing with my plants and could only chuckle when I'd hear about husband-and-wife arguments over how to tend their yards. Luckily for me, Michael hated yard work and had no interest in gardening. I'd later come to see that Manny, like me, liked control over the yards he tended and that he and I might ultimately lock horns in power struggles over my yard.

Manny was a serious dude, very focused on his work, and proud of his good results. Carmen's outstanding physical characteristic was her big, warm smile.

Early on, I realized my questions and comments should go to Manny rather than to Carmen. I also noticed that Manny didn't always agree with comments I'd make. He would visibly bristle when I'd ask questions like why everyone in the neighborhood had their azaleas and rhododendrons trimmed into Christmas balls. As for the fairytale appearance of the Dr. Seuss shrubbery in the neighborhood, or why all the yards seemed almost indistinguishable from each other, Manny acted as if he thought I was crazy when I asked him about it. "That's the way it's done around here," he said.

Well, I thought. Maybe guerrilla gardening will become my thing. Gardening as a political act of protest. Already, Michael and I were finding ourselves bristling at some of the many rules and regulations in this manicured neighborhood. "What have we done?" I asked rhetorically, several times a day. Neither of us knew.

We had moved into our house in late summer, when temperatures occasionally reached triple digits. Plants were alive because of inground sprinkler systems, and thick wildfire smoke turned outside activities into health hazards. We were so busy settling into our house I hardly thought about the yard except to note Manny's twice-monthly services. And to pay him, of course.

In the beginning, I paid Manny through PayPal. I loved that arrangement since my credit card earned me frequent flyer miles with Southwest. Then he informed me he was shutting down his PayPal account and I'd need to write a check each month. I wasn't pleased with this old-fashioned payment method, and Manny's was usually the only check I wrote each month.

While far from exuding any curb appeal, our yard didn't violate our neighborhood's high standards with its artificial, manicured look. Manny kept the azaleas and rhododendrons appropriately rounded, and the boxwoods and junipers squared up evenly with the sidewalk and driveway.

When the shorter days, winter rains, and cooler temperatures arrived, I began seriously surveying my yard and fantasizing possibilities. Could I possibly turn this place into something artsy and funky and fun? My neighbors encouraged me to garden, promising that almost anything I planted would double in size in the first year.

I was on fire with big plans for my future yard. I knew I needed to be careful not to upset or offend Manny, since he'd be the brawn for many of the planned projects that I physically lacked the strength to do. While I wasn't pleased to be dependent on a gardener, at least I had one to help me.

I came to realize that yard services were hard to come by in this neighborhood. The existing crews had all the work they could manage, and most were not accepting new customers. It behooved me to get along with Manny. I began to pay more attention to my p's and q's. If I lost Manny's services, I'd be high and dry in a neighborhood that didn't tolerate unkempt yards.

OVER-55 Conniptions

I hated that I'd gotten so old I could no longer maintain a yard by myself. Maybe if this had been an established yard that halfway pleased me, I'd have been able to manage. But I had big dreams, a medium-sized brain, and very limited brawn.

CHAPTER 17

Should I Be Doing This?

"Are you okay? Let me help you up." My friend Chloe, a good ten years younger than I, extended her hand to help me up from the curb where I'd just toppled over. My bicycle had landed on top of me. We were on Main Street in Springfield, trying to find our way back to the bike trail that would take us to Clearwater Park, five or six miles to the east.

What the hell? I thought. Did I trip over my foot? How did I get down here? We'd been crossing the street when Chloe noted there was not a bike lane. She'd stopped to ask if I wanted to try the street anyway or maybe walk the bikes on the sidewalk until we found a safer route. I fell before having a chance to answer.

"I can get it," I said, horrified at my predicament. I didn't want my friend to see my bloody hand, so I tried to keep it out of her sight. I was glad to have worn long pants; I was sure my right knee was also bleeding. I squirmed away from the bike and slowly stood, chagrined at having had to get on all fours like a toddler to stand up. My artificial knees didn't bend like real knees, leaving me feeling like a ridiculous old woman. Which I was. Whatever had possessed me to buy a bicycle at my age? I wondered if I hadn't made a horrible miscalculation in my seventy-five-year-old abilities and agilities.

I'd only had my new Trek Verve 2 for a couple of weeks. It was yet another loopy decision I'd made recently, a pathetic attempt to defy the aging process. I wanted to give time the finger. I wanted to believe that just because I was seventy-five, it did not mean I was deteriorating and on my way to the grave. Taking up bicycling at my age was yet another temper tantrum to protest the inevitable. At least I'd go out having fun.

I cringed to think I might have broken a bone with my fall. I, like many of my contemporaries, feared broken bones like the plague. From what I'd seen, a fall often signaled the beginning of an end game. I personally knew a couple of folks who'd fallen, broken hips, and never walked again. Those were not the kind of twilight years I wanted for myself. But then, I'm sure no one would.

About a week later, I plunked over again. This time I was in a bike lane at a busy intersection, sandwiched between a car going straight and a car turning right. The light turned green, and as I began to push off, I lost my balance and fell. Adrenaline undoubtedly fueled my rapid recovery as I scrambled, impressively for an old woman like me, to my feet. The driver on my right rolled down his window to ask if I was alright, and I assured him I was.

My new bicycle felt heavy and unwieldy. While considered a hybrid, it looked more like a beach cruiser than the sleek, ultra-light racer I'd fantasized riding. At least it wasn't turquoise or pink with plastic flowers woven into a wicker basket in front, which would have been a frilly, girly image I'd not want to project. One of my most frequent alter ego fantasies while riding was that of being an elite athlete despite eschewing an expensive, fashionable wardrobe of kits and cleats. I hated the distance between my inflated, exaggerated self-image and the suspicion of how others viewed my old-woman self.

My clunker bicycle weighed 28.7 pounds, per the manufacturer, but that was before adding accessories. Fenders seemed important since this was the rainy Pacific Northwest and I wanted to avoid stripes down my back from riding on wet roads or through unavoidable puddles. I added a rearview mirror, for safety, since my neck was arthritic and my head couldn't turn as far as it once did. I added lights in both the front and the rear to increase my visibility and reduce the likelihood I'd get killed by a distracted motorist who happened to be texting. I added a computer since I tend to be obsessive about time, distance, and speed when I ride. I'd added a rear trunk in which I carried an index card with emergency contact information, a twenty-dollar bill for emergencies, a spare tube and small air pump in case of blowouts, a water repellant jacket in case of rain, a couple of boxes of raisins and one granola bar for low blood sugar emergencies, a bicycle lock in case I decided to go into a store or restaurant, and an extra bottle of water in case I got stranded and drank all the water from the bottle attached to the bicycle frame. With all these accessories and supplies, the loaded bike probably weighed thirty-five pounds or more. I wistfully thought of the YouTube videos I'd seen of women lifting ultralight carbon-framed bikes with two fingers. Too bad I was such a cheapskate and unwilling to spend five or six thousand dollars on such a bike.

I didn't draw blood during this second fall, but I did get a couple of new bruises. They somehow blended right in to all my other bruises and scrapes, some from bicycling but most from gardening. I began to reevaluate the safety of bicycle riding. I'd previously thought the major risk had to do with vehicles hitting me. I was beginning to realize I possibly posed more danger to myself than all those cars and trucks out there combined.

In time, I magically seemed to learn how to stay upright on the damned thing. Within a few months, I even managed to ride through the spot of my second fall without having a near-panic attack that it'd happen again. I've yet to go riding again with Chloe. Maybe if I wait long enough before inviting her again, she'll have forgotten about my klutzy fall. Or perhaps she was so embarrassed for me that she was afraid to ask me to go bicycling with her again.

The greatest challenge of bicycling, however, has not been staying upright but rather the challenges of flat tires. The first flat happened on my third day of bicycle ownership when I had less than twenty-five miles on my odometer. An RVing friend, Brad, was in town and he wanted to show me the River Trail along the Willamette River. When I walked into the garage about an hour before he was due to arrive, I discovered a flat tire on my bike.

Brad went with me to Walmart to buy a new tube and then coached me through changing the flat. Despite my feminist leanings, I'd found myself wishing Brad would just be a gentleman and change the damned tire for me. I really didn't like getting my hands dirty (except when I gardened), plus this tire-changing business made the arthritis in my hands hurt. But I persevered and tried not to embarrass myself too much. All was good.

I viewed that flat tire as a fluke and didn't give it another thought. Until two weeks later, when I had a second flat, also on the rear. Brad had left the area, leaving me on my own this time. I was about five miles from home when the tire went flat, but luckily at a spot along the river trail where Michael could find me. I called him, but of course my hubby didn't answer his phone. After trying for several frustrating minutes to reach him, I finally called my friend two houses down and asked her to go bang on our door and tell Michael to call me.

Fifteen minutes later, Michael pulled up to the trail in the car. I loaded the bike on the rack, and after dropping Michael off at home, I drove directly to the bike shop to express my exasperation over two flat tires in two weeks. The tech in the shop changed the tire but failed to find anything in either the tire or the tube that could have caused the flat.

The next flat was on the front and happened about a month later. It occurred close to home, and I walked the mile or so rather than bothering Michael. Again, I took the bike to the shop for repair. This time the tech showed me a sliver of metal embedded in the tire that had punctured the tube. Had this flat occurred on the back tire, I would have sworn that something had jinxed my bike, and I would have screamed for a full refund. Despite the near hysteria of a third flat in less than two months, I maintained control. The tech and a salesperson were almost ingratiating as they assured me flat tires were common in Eugene.

By this point, I would do everything short of Duct-taping Michael's phone to his clothes before I'd go out riding. He was notorious for losing his phone, not keeping it with him, letting the battery go dead, not checking for messages, failing to return calls or texts, and all kinds of other communication breakdowns. For me, my phone was an extension of myself, with me always and checked multiple times every hour.

Flat tire number four proved so unsurprising I hardly winced. It happened on the front again, and this time the shop tech found both a sliver of glass and a piece of metal. I'm not sure how to explain my equanimity in the face of this ongoing, increasingly expensive and time-consuming problem of flat tires.

Flat tire number five happened on my three-month, three-day anniversary of bicycle ownership, and this time my disgust bordered on hysteria. "This bike is jinxed," I announced as I once again wheeled my piece-of-crap bike through the store to the repair station in the back. Had the young men in the shop not been so nice and solicitous, I might have gone ballistic. Instead of screaming or crying, I politely asked, "How much money would I lose if I traded this thing in on another bike? This one doesn't seem to be working out very well for me."

"You'd lose a lot," the tech said, with a strong emphasis on the word 'lot.' "Let's take a look." This time he found another glass sliver.

"I don't understand," I said. "I mostly ride on the trail, and I never see broken glass there. And on the street, I constantly watch the ground and avoid debris. I just can't believe this keeps happening to me."

"Oh, the trails are pretty bad, especially under the bridges," the tech said. "I got a flat four days ago and found a hypodermic needle in my tire. Flats happen all the time, and Fall is the worst time." This was mid-October. He recommended I upgrade my tires to a puncture-resistant set. I agreed, feeling that I'd recoup the $125 cost in less than six months if I continued at my current rate of flat tires.

I could easily believe the tech's report of the hypodermic needle puncture, and it gave me yet something else to worry. The local park service had built this bike trail, which ran for miles on both banks of the Willamette River, on protected public lands which they'd left wooded and natural. It provided a desirable location for Eugene's large population of unhoused people to pitch tents and construct lean-tos in places with thick vegetation. Such tent communities were especially popular in the less-used northern parts of the trail, where I most often entered and exited.

Five pedestrian and three vehicle bridges cross the river, and the underpasses of these bridges offered protection from the elements. I'd often ride past groups of congregated folks, usually men. Because the underpasses were in deep shade, I'd sometimes not realize there were people underneath them until I reached the entrance. I could easily imagine a hypodermic needle under one of these shelters.

As my cycling months added up, I realized that every two to three months authorities slapped eviction notices on the fronts of the tents of the homeless. Within a couple of days, most all the residents had packed up their belongings in wagons, shopping carts, or whatever else kind of wheeled conveyances they'd managed to find and moved on. Invariably, they left huge piles of garbage behind, and it'd usually take several weeks for cleanup crews to haul it all away. A short time later, another batch of unhoused people would set up their tents.

At first, I felt vulnerable and exposed as I'd ride through these tent-populated areas. If something happened to me, there'd be no one who could hear my screams or come to my rescue. I hated that I felt scared. As a social worker, I thought I had a better than average understanding of the myriad factors that can lead to homelessness. I wished the compassion and concern in my heart would drown out my fear.

Eventually, my self talk worked. I convinced myself that riding through dark tunnels with strangers doing God-only-knows-what was probably safer than riding down Crescent Avenue with crazy texting drivers or falling over in the middle of intersections or even getting stranded for hours somewhere with a flat tire because my husband wouldn't pick up the phone and come to my rescue.

Of course, I could solve the flat tire problem and the need for hubby to come get me if I'd just get off my princess throne, aka my lazy Prima Donna butt, and change my own flat tires. Maybe I'll do that in time, but not yet.

CHAPTER 18

Building New Lives

How many times in life can one start over? When we first started RVing, the lifestyle change felt huge. Prior to RVing, a vacation for us would last two or three weeks at most. Now we were taking six-month long trips, and the motorhome started to feel as much like home as our sticks-and-bricks house in Tampa. In retrospect, those early RV trips made the transition to full time almost like a nonevent. I never looked back, and I never missed the house or anything in it. Although I missed friends, neighbors, and gardening, I thought I could live a minimalistic lifestyle in an RV forever.

Once we bought a house in Eugene, I was amazed at how easily I made the transition back to sticks-and-bricks. Somehow, we emptied the motorhome and set up housekeeping without missing a beat. Physically, life was much easier in a house than in an RV. No longer did I have to deal with meltdowns in a new grocery store for not being able to find the damn Cheerios or end up driving fifteen minutes trying to find a Shell station for gas. Within a few months, we knew our way around town and even a couple of shortcuts, usually without using the GPS. It helped that we switched from Cheerios to oatmeal for breakfast and quickly learned our way around our new WinCo supermarket. With Cosco a half mile from our house, we never stopped at another Shell station for gas. Life almost seemed a bit too easy in the beginning.

I was thrilled to have a garden again and went overboard with planning, planting, and admiring. I could have spent days on end in my yard, talking only occasionally with neighbors walking up and down the sidewalk as they made their daily afternoon treks to get their mail. If I wasn't in the mood to talk, which was often, I stayed in the backyard out of sight.

I joined a couple of writers' groups and met people there. Unfortunately, gardening trumped writing for me. My writing muse appeared to have gone into hibernation when we parked the RV at a storage facility, since travel had been my primary writing topic. Other writing distractions included the chaotic events unfolding in the world such as climate change disasters, the war in the Ukraine, political turmoil around the world and in the United States, multiple felony charges filed against a former President in a country where two totally incompatible truths existed, and then the eruption of war between Israel and Hamas in the Gaza Strip. Covid had resolved to the point that no one seemed to worry about dying anymore, while these other occurrences left me feeling the world could end at any moment, so what was the point?

With so many troubling things going on in the world, and with settling into our new house, it took over a year before I settled down enough to sit at my laptop several hours a day to write. It's hard for connections with other writers to go anywhere if one is not writing herself. So much for those early attempts at immersing myself in the local writing scene.

Bicycling got me out of the house and out of the garden with the added advantage of giving me an activity away from Michael. After living full time in such tight quarters in an RV for almost three years, it felt good to have space apart, which we agreed was healthy and normal. Besides which, the long, wet, cold winters would give us more than enough cooped-up time together inside our house.

Michael is the extrovert in our family, and he loves to be out and about, especially socializing and listening to live music. We joined a local wine club and began to make friends there. The wine club proved to be a wonderful venue for live music, with local musicians playing two-hour gigs three or four times a week, usually from six to eight p.m. This was perfect for old geezers like us who didn't want to drive home in the dark. That red wine was my drink of choice made this membership even more fortuitous and fun.

We also started going to a local blues venue, where we developed another set of friends, these in our age bracket of late sixties and early to mid-seventies. Our wine bar buddies were mostly in their fifties, and we felt flattered that these folks who were young enough to be our children had accepted us as their friends.

We had several other various and assorted friends not associated with either the blues bar or the wine club. There were my two bicycling buddies, Brad and Chloe. I had a couple of friends I'd met at writers' meetings. We had a family of three we'd met at an RV park who'd now settled in Eugene, just as we had. Gradually, we were building our new lives from what felt like nothing. The combination of plopping down in a new town after riding out a two-year pandemic in near isolation had left us feeling bereft of significant relationships. We embraced every new acquaintance who even marginally presented as a potential friend.

I wish I could say we acquired new social contacts in Spring Hill at the same acquisition rate as in the community, but alas, we did not. Michael and I were amazed to see how few of our new neighbors seemed to ever get out of their houses. For the two monthly social events in the community clubhouse, i.e. a Saturday morning coffee hour and a Friday night dinner, the same twenty-five or thirty folks showed up over and over. This small turnout came from a community of over 150 residents. In the early months in Spring Hill, Michael and I faithfully made the clubhouse trek to attend the functions, but we found cliques, and our new neighbors did not seem especially friendly toward us. After a few months, we stopped going, which did nothing to help our acceptance and welcome into the neighborhood.

Gardening seemed to be the only topic I'd found to talk about with the few neighbors who left their homes to walk around the community. I started attending a monthly garden club meeting in the clubhouse on Thursday afternoons. The unorganized group met for an hour, and the format was to go around the circle with each of the attendees talking for a few minutes about what was going on in their yard. After a few months, I felt accepted and began getting to know a few neighbors a bit better.

Despite our growing number of friends, it didn't feel like our social life jelled because all our "friends" fell into such disparate categories and groups. It began to feel like we had several circles. Were we to visualize these circles as Venn Diagrams, there'd be very little overlap. We hosted a party at our house in September, sort of a one-year celebration of Eugene residency. We invited our wine bar friends, our Mac's blues club friends, the few folks we'd gotten to know in our neighborhood, and the handful of various and sundry folks we'd met at other places, for a total of about thirty people. While the party seemed to go well, our neighbors hovered on the outside patio, our wine bar friends were on the porch, and our blues bar friends sat inside in the living room.

"Well, that was interesting," was about all I could find to say to Michael the following day.

He agreed.

The honeymoon with our new hometown, house, and friends lasted about a year before I realized we'd made some mistakes along the way. At first, I thought it just had to do with some of the furniture and home furnishings we'd bought in the first couple of months in the new house. We were starting anew, with very few possessions still in a storage facility in Florida. We needed bedroom furniture, living room furniture, and a place to sit down to eat, at a minimum. We bought a new bedroom set, including a Tempur-Pedic mattress, for the bedroom. Everything else we bought from consignment and thrift stores.

"I really don't care what it looks like," I blithely said to Michael. "It's silly to have to buy all this stuff. We lived for three years with so little. This is not how I want to live."

"Well, Little Gerri, I'm not much happier about this than you are."

I was in the same predicament I'd been in in 2019 when the idea of going full time first arose. Back then, I wanted to chuck it all and become a nomad with all my heart and soul, to the same extent that I wanted to stay home and tend to the 200 orchids growing on my lanai. I reconciled the incompatible choices by telling myself the decision was not irreversible. I was seventy-two and Michael was seventy when we took off on the road. We both knew at the time that we were a bit old to be doing this and that our nomad days were finite. Still, having medical issues become the determining factor was a bitter pill to swallow.

It was a boondoggle of emotions, this whole business of coming in from the cold. On one hand, there was pride that we'd made it so long, that we'd had those incredible adventures and seen things that most folks only dreamed of seeing in their lifetimes, that we'd managed to stay on the road long enough to remain proactive about where and how to live, and that we'd picked what we still considered the perfect place to live.

On the other hand, we now found ourselves surrounded by Oregonians who'd lived in Eugene for most of their lives. We had neighbors who had gone to elementary school together. We were and would probably always be outsiders, no matter how long we lived here. I found it disconcerting to look around and realize Michael was the only soul in all of Oregon, the entire West Coast actually, who knew or cared about any of my history. It suddenly felt like an overwhelming loss to no longer have a past that anyone knew or appreciated.

On a positive note, however, I once again had an opportunity to redefine myself, to start over, to become anything and anybody I wanted to be. I'd started over a couple of times already in life. This time would likely be the last time, so I knew I'd better make it good. Which meant that second-guessing, whining, and complaining were not options. I knew I needed to get my act together, to adjust to this old folks' community, and make myself fit in. I needed to treat this current opportunity with sacred reverence.

CHAPTER 19

Maybe I'll Become a Dating Coach

You need a mail order bride from Thailand; I sighed in response to Jeremy's latest Facebook post in which he expressed two major complaints about his online social life. First, he bemoaned all the beautiful young women responding to his online dating profile whom he could never meet because of the geographical distance. Second, he expressed dismay that most of the beautiful women who'd responded to his ad eventually wanted either money or to sell him cryptocurrency.

Beautiful. Young. Women. Were these really the most important characteristics my friend Jeremy sought in a girlfriend/future wife? As my mother used to say when she'd get riled up about something, "It makes me so mad I could spit nails." I was less than two swallows away from spitting.

Even my oft-oblivious husband Michael took note of Jeremy's post. "Bet that's going to piss off a few women." He looked up at me from his iPad and grinned. "Yep. I can tell it didn't sit well with you."

"If I thought he'd understand, I'd tell him how his post made me feel."

"He wouldn't know what you were talking about."

"Agreed." Somehow Jeremy seemed unaware that there'd been a feminist awakening several decades ago, or maybe he just hadn't been exposed to women with attitudes like mine and the women I hung out with. I couldn't imagine it could be a case of him not caring. Even though prone to occasional blind spots, most of my men friends were aware that women didn't appreciate men viewing them as objects.

Norma Jean and I had been close, but as I thought back, I realized we'd never talked about women's issues and gender equality. She often spoke of her relationship with Jeremy, how they always made joint decisions, and how wonderful it was to have such a kind and gentle partner. She told me her first husband had been abusive. But how had she really seen Jeremy? Could Jeremy have been a closet chauvinist who hid it well in public? No, that thought did not ring true.

Initially, I thought Jeremy's filters might be a bit faulty, that maybe he didn't know which thoughts were okay to share and which he should keep private. But that didn't ring true either.

I need to cut my friend some slack, I thought. It's not fair to feel perturbed at someone going through such a significant and painful loss as Jeremy. I'd never experienced anything comparable and had trouble even imagining what it must feel like to be in Jeremy's shoes.

"I want to introduce Jeremy to Brad," I said to Michael. "They'd have some things in common. Both are RVers, and they're about the same age. But Brad seems happy being alone while Jeremy is tunnel-visioned to find a wife."

"Not a bad idea to introduce them. Brad did have that Leadville woman he almost married though."

"But Brad wasn't desperate, and the way I remember the story, he's the one that didn't follow-up with her."

I texted Brad, coordinated with Jeremy, and set a time to get together. Brad had lived, raised two sons, and worked for years in Eugene. He still had a wide network of friends and acquaintances in the area, making it hard for him to squeeze us in. But maybe just as much a factor, Brad liked spending time alone. He bicycled, kayaked, and hiked. He had a life, and I wanted Jeremy to see this.

"Barbecued chicken and all the sides," I promised Jeremy and Brad, "and maybe we'll throw darts on the back porch if it's not too hot."

Brad and Jeremy seemed to like each other well enough, although Jeremy did not reveal his online dating activities and wife-procurement goal. As we were clearing dishes from the table in preparation for dessert, Brad brought up the subject of his lost Leadville opportunity. "She wasn't really from Leadville," he explained. "She was writing a book set in Leadville, so that's why I called her that. I'd hoped to find her here in Eugene, since she's usually here in the summer." He went on to explain how he'd totally misunderstood how serious she'd been about their relationship. He now realized she'd cut him out of her life forever in disgust because of his reluctance to commit. "I was ready to get down on my hands and knees and beg her to take me back, but now she won't even talk to me anymore."

As Jeremy and Brad were leaving, Brad called back to me, "Now don't forget that I'd like to meet some of those single women I keep seeing in your Facebook posts. I'd love to find a nice grandma."

So much for Brad's rich and full life, I thought.

Is my life going to end up with ongoing bombardment by lonely men seeking female companionship? Here I'd thought Brad would be the perfect role model for someone like Jeremy. I guessed I didn't know Brad as well as I'd thought I had. Still, it impressed me that Brad had enough self-awareness and insight to reflect on a past relationship and realize that he'd failed to pick up on cues as to what his Leadville girlfriend had wanted.

I wondered if Jeremy ever engaged in a similar examination of his own role in the outcomes of his dating efforts. He had told Michael and me about several potential dates, only to later report that the meetups never happened. I felt deeply immersed in this dating odyssey with Jeremy, and felt awful for him that so far, he'd had only one date with any of those beautiful women whose glamour-shot photos he viewed on his dating sites. And this date was not even one that he initiated, which in retrospect should have made him suspicious from the beginning.

Per Jeremy, an attractive woman in her mid-forties from one of his online dating sites initiated the materialized rendezvous. She explained that she lived in California but visited her sister here in Eugene on a regular basis and wondered if he would like to meet her for dinner at the Gordon Hotel, a nice, upscale hotel and restaurant in the downtown area. Jeremy accepted, and they reportedly had a pleasant dinner. As they finished their meals, the woman asked him to get a room in the hotel, at a cost of $250 for the night, so they could "have some time together."

"I realized then," Jeremy said, "that she was a prostitute. When I said 'no,' I didn't want to get a room, she got angry and stormed off."

I can get frustrated at men for falling for this kind of crap, but I can get just as upset at the women who start it. Maybe I ought to become a dating coach like the one that Jeremy hired. I felt in my gut that this coach was a charlatan, and I didn't believe for a New York minute that he'd helped Jeremy one iota.

If I were a dating coach, I'd advise folks to 'run like hell' from online dating sites. Further advice might be: If you're mourning the loss of a partner from either divorce or death, do not try to find a replacement until you've reached a point of acceptance and are completely happy with the new life you've crafted for yourself. You're not ready to enter a relationship until you're happy on the inside. Then, do not go out searching for love. Focus on making friends, for the best way of meeting appropriate potential partners is through friends and acquaintances. Meeting strangers is quasi-acceptable only if someone you know and trust has arranged the blind date.

How easy it would be to navigate the singles world, I tell myself, gloating in my self-righteousness. The only thing I need to validate my brilliant insights is a little pain and loneliness, eh? But then, I doubt any of those life coaches or dating coaches have a clue what it feels like to lose a spouse of several decades. Just like I don't know and am obnoxious to think I might have an inkling of what it would feel like.

Forgive me, Jeremy, for my snarky judgmental attitudes.

CHAPTER 20

Trying to Fit In

We began to meet more of our new neighbors, albeit not nearly as fast as we would've liked. The ones from the monthly Saturday morning coffees and the Friday night dinners never developed into anything more than "Hey, how are you doing?" kinds of relationships.

"This place surely has a lot of cliques, doesn't it?" I asked Michael one morning after our return from one of the coffee hours. "Did anyone talk with you?"

"Only that new couple with the guy in the wheelchair, and I think that was only because he couldn't find another place to sit."

"I don't think we're fitting in very well here, do you?"

"You need to learn to knit. Then you could join that group of women who get together every Wednesday afternoon to gossip for two hours while doing their little stitchery, crafty things."

"Well, I'm not sure they gossip. That's not a very nice thing to say," I said. But I knew I'd never join that group. All those yarn and thread projects—knitting, embroidery, crocheting, needle-punch, and other homemaker type projects took me back to my childhood. My mother had insisted I learn all those domestic skills, and by the time I was ten years old, I was furiously embroidering tablecloths and dinner napkins to go in my Hope Chest. I grew up hearing all the women in the neighborhood saying to me and my friends, "Someday you'll be wives and mothers, and you should know how to do these things."

One day I hope I'll stop bristling from all the careers that might have been available to me if only I'd known they existed. It's wrong to feel resentful though. None of those advice-givers back then could have imagined the freedom I would eventually eke out for myself. It even stuns me a bit sometimes how far I've come as the daughter of a share-cropping farmer with a seventh-grade education and a mother from the backwoods of South Georgia who married on the day she graduated high school. I ended up getting married on the same day I received my Bachelor's degree, albeit inadvertently. I used to tell my daughter she could marry on the day she received her Ph.D., but she didn't listen.

Mildred, who appeared to be the head honcho for clubhouse gatherings, approached me shortly after we moved in and asked if I'd like to be on the social committee. I said yes, thinking it would jumpstart my acceptance into the community. For the first three months that we lived in Spring Hill, I worked like a peon in the kitchen helping with the setups and the cleanups for the coffees and dinners.

While I dutifully attended monthly social committee meetings with Mildred and my next-door neighbor Mary Lou, I never seemed to rise above the status of direction follower. After a few months, I begged off, saying I had other plans when contacted for my volunteer shifts. It didn't take long for Mildred to drop me from the social committee's list of invitees for their meetings, and I didn't blame them one bit. I handled the situation badly. But in my defense, I felt like I'd been working my butt off and making no progress whatsoever toward getting to know people any better or making friends.

🛺

Spring Hill has a large, old-fashioned bulletin board under the shelter at the community mailboxes. It's as low tech as anything could be, with a little cup sitting on the bench below holding pencils and ballpoint pens. The bulletin board has pushpins stuck in the cork for folks to pin up notices or index cards with messages. Committee leaders post signup sheets so people can sign up for various activities, such as the monthly Friday night dinners, the talk by the Eugene Police Depart on how to avoid getting scammed on the internet, or the guy from the fire department telling us what we should be doing protect ourselves from burning to a crisp should we have a fire inside our house.

We were glad we attended the Fire Marshall's talk. When we returned home and dutifully checked the dates on the fire extinguishers that came with our house, we found they'd both expired in 1992. Those two fire extinguishers had expired thirty years ago! So much for the previous owners staying on top of things. I'm just glad we caught it and were able to rush to Home Depot to buy new ones. Now I only needed to figure out how Michael and I could get out the window in our bedroom without killing ourselves should there be a fire at night in the kitchen or in the pantry where the fuse box is located.

A local for-profit independent living/assisted living/nursing home corporation presented a program in our clubhouse that surprised me. Its stated goal was to help us in planning for our futures. I couldn't help but think that some of these folks in Spring Hill should move at lightning speed while they still could. Overhearing conversations at the mailboxes, I wryly noted that folks seemed to appreciate that this corporation was being so helpful. Didn't they realize the corporation was coming to hopefully make money off us poor, trusting old souls? There'd be no money to make from me, however, since you could not have paid me to sit through a talk like that.

In fairness and with full disclosure, however, I admit the problem was not the Spring Hill committee that scheduled the presentation nor the corporation that came to speak. The problem was me. I was not ready to face that kind of planning yet. I'd just come in from being a nomad, feeling like the wind had been kicked out of me due to health issues, primarily Michael's, and I simply was not ready to consider yet another chapter in my life that would require more changes. My goal at that time was to stay in my little manufactured home until I dropped dead, preferably suddenly and painlessly. (I'd later realize that at this point in my Spring Hill residency, I still had my head buried deep in the sand. Today

I might have gone down to hear what those corporation representatives had to say.)

I did check out one regularly scheduled event held at the clubhouse—a monthly garden club meeting. Very loosely organized and informal, residents sat around a big square table. After some initial chitchat, they'd go around the room and each person would talk for a few minutes about what they were doing in their gardens, problems they were having, and perhaps ask the group for advice or recommendations. I found both the group and the format helpful and fun. I credit my participation in this group for moving a couple of steps closer to feeling accepted. It was the one place and the one small group of people with whom I felt comradery. Some of these folks were even more enthusiastic about their gardening than I was, and all of them knew more about gardening in Eugene than I did. I began to feel like I might eventually find a kindred soul somewhere in this place.

Sarah was the leader of the garden club when I first started attending. She had retired from the Lane County Extension Service where she'd worked for years as a secretary. She had raved about the Master Gardeners the first time I met her but then shot me right down at my first meeting by telling me anything I thought I might know about gardening wouldn't work here. In retrospect, I made a grave error when I mentioned that I'd been a Master Gardener in Florida during that first meeting. From then on, Sarah seemed to love saying to me, at every chance she got, "You just need to forget all about the gardening you did in Florida. It's different here." I never failed to bristle. Yes, I certainly understood there was some truth in her statement. But I also understood the discipline of researching plants before buying them, the importance of not putting a ten-dollar plant in a two-dollar hole (my mom always told me to put ten-dollar plants in twenty-dollar holes), and other gardening truths that transcend soil, climate, and selection, such as the extra care all plants need until they become established. I knew how to grow plants.

I kept my fingers crossed that Sarah would be around long enough to see my blasé yard transformed into something stunning. Despite all the semi-veiled criticisms I'd received so far on my yard and my plant choices, I stayed optimistic that in time I'd have a yard I'd be proud of.

But Sarah would possibly never get to see that. I first learned of her difficulties when I saw a small notice posted on the community bulletin board saying that doctors had released her from the hospital and transferred her to a rehab center.

I stopped my friend Polly on the sidewalk a couple of days later to ask what the story was with Sarah. Polly seemed to know all the neighborhood news since she went to both the weekly Tai Chi and the line dancing classes.

"She fell on her patio and broke her leg," Polly said. "The worst thing is that her little dog, Daisy, that she adopted just a few months ago, is miserable. It had been a rescue but has really bonded with Sarah, and now the dog is there by herself. I hear that Sarah worries more about the dog than she does herself." Polly went on to explain that neighbors walked and fed the dog, sometimes even went to Sarah's house just to sit with the dog a while to provide companionship.

I'd seen Sarah walking that little dog. Although walking slowly with a cane, she trudged around the block and passed my house every afternoon with Daisy on a leash. I remember thinking it was good that the dog was so small and that it seemed to walk well on a leash. A tugging, straining dog, even one as small as Daisy, could have toppled frail Sarah right to the ground.

In time, Sarah managed to graduate from rehab and return home. She took her place at the head of the garden club meeting table one more time before her relapse. At this meeting, she excitedly shared her rehab story with the group.

"The most exciting thing happened," Sarah said. "There were five of us there who really hit it off and would hang out together during the day, in-between all the therapies and stuff they had us doing." Her speech was rapid and animated, and I couldn't help but notice the twinkle in her eyes. "Well, one of the people in the group was this guy, a couple of years younger than I, and he and I just really hit it off. We became so close that we could talk about anything." She went on to say he'd been in rehab for over a year because he had nowhere else to go and no family or close friends who could help him. "Everyone he knew had passed away already, so he was really alone in this world."

Garden club members listened attentively, perhaps as mesmerized as I by Sarah's story. A couple of her friends asked questions that served to keep her talking.

"We finally realized that in another lifetime, he and I could have been soulmates, like married happily to each other forever. His wife had died ten years ago, my husband seven." Sarah shook her head, and I swear I saw tears well in her eyes. "I wish I could bring him to my house, but I'm not able to take care of him. The best I'll be able to do is visit him as soon as I'm able to drive again."

Unfortunately, that day never came for Sarah. The surgical wound from her broken leg became infected, and she was in and out of the hospital for several months with a wound that refused to heal. A caregiver moved into her house to be with Daisy and to care for Sarah when she was at home. In just a couple of months, however, Sarah had to move to assisted living. The word on the street was that Sarah refused to put her house on the market to sell because she really wanted to come back to Spring Hill. The scuttlebutt was also that Sarah would never be able to step into her home again. A year and a half later, Sarah remained in rehab and her house continued to sit empty. She reportedly continued to refuse to sell the house because of her dream of returning home.

I could certainly identify with Sarah's predicament. My Mohs surgical wound from almost two years earlier had still not healed properly, but at least I'd managed to avoid infections and hospitalizations. Better yet, I was still on my feet with no limitations on daily activities and with no apparent impact on my overall health and wellbeing.

I thought about Sarah's story often. She was the second Spring Hill resident to leave the neighborhood whom I'd known personally.

The neighborhood seemed to shrug about both Eleanor and Sarah's exits, and since then I've seen several other houses vacated, sold, and with new people moving in shortly after. Some departing residents passed away, others went to facilities, and the rest moved away, often to be closer to adult children. It brought home to me what a revolving gate all of us Spring Hill residents lived behind. I rarely heard the names Eleanor or Sarah mentioned again after they moved. Likely typical for every Spring Hillian who'd left, it was an out of sight, out of mind situation.

But maybe residents here in Spring Hill didn't talk about Eleanor and Sarah because it was just all too painful. In many ways, every resident's exit served as a blaring, blatant wakeup call that it would happen to every one of us living here in this damnable over-55 community. At some point, there'd probably be an estate sale at my house, with strangers pawing and grabbing at my half-empty salt shaker or dead potted plants because they wanted the nice planters.

My insight made me wonder, too, if part of the "unfriendliness" of this neighborhood was a reluctance to form new relationships when the likelihood of them lasting very long was slim. How many goodbyes to friends should any individual have to say? How many neighbors would I watch decline and ultimately leave before I didn't want to see it anymore?

I confess to becoming a little less outgoing and friendly myself. Remembering that my wine bar friends were in their fifties was very reassuring to me. I figured the odds were slim that those fifty-year-olds would be dying off or moving into care facilities anytime soon.

Maybe not fitting into this neighborhood wasn't such a bad thing after all.

Two years after that assisted living placement, Sarah returned home. While in a wheelchair and with a fulltime caregiver, Sarah moved back into the house and community she loved so much. Neighbors were hesitant to predict Sarah's chances of lasting very long back in Spring Hill; I think they realized, just as I did, that one should never say never. We were right not to celebrate too early. Sarah was in her house only a few months before distant relatives in California learned of her medical issues and her isolation from kin. These kind relatives moved Sarah to a facility near their home so they could visit. In its own way, Sarah's story had two heartwarming endings—Sarah's return to her own home and the reunification with long-lost family. It's not that often that one hears heartwarming stories in Spring Hill.

I don't know what happened to Sarah's little rescue named Daisy. And I've forgiven Sarah for her constant intimations that the gardening skills I brought with me from Florida were worthless for gardening in Oregon.

CHAPTER 21

Elite Cyclists Don't Topple Over

There were a couple of other cyclists in Spring Hill, but I thought for months that I was the only woman. Then I learned the one elite-looking cyclist in the neighborhood was female. It's sometimes hard to tell. How proud I felt to be out there riding, usually four or five days a week. And how pretentious I knew I was, referring to myself as a cyclist.

The cyclist I mistook for a woman was a very tall, thin rider who dressed to the nines in flashy, color-coordinated kits, shoes, socks, and helmet. Her bicycle looked like one from the Tour de France. I'm certain the bike had a carbon frame and was at least a $5000 purchase, maybe even double that. I'm also thinking that if the folks who considered themselves 'the enforcers of rules' in this neighborhood had radar guns, they might have been able to bust her for speeding. The park is a big circle with one short street going down the middle and then three short streets with cul-de-sacs near the entrance. I did not know where this speed demon lived, but by the time she flew by my house, it looked like her speed was up to at least 20 mph. The speed limit is 15 mph, so I'm thinking a couple of fuddy-duddies watched this possible rulebreaker from their kitchen windows in horror.

The other cyclist was Don, a very friendly and funny guy who rode a hybrid that looked like a cross between a recumbent and a road bike.

The frame was long from front to back, stretched like a limousine, and slightly lower to the ground than a regular bike. Because of the bike's unique design, Don had explained to me, he and his wife had to buy a bike rack for their car that held three bicycles for the infrequent occasions when they transported their two bikes out of the subdivision. Don's bike was turquoise in color, and he always wore a bright yellow windbreaker when he took his daily rides.

Although the winters here in the Pacific Northwest are typically dark, rainy, and cold, usually there'd be a break in the rain at some point during the day, and this is when Don would make his move. I'm not sure he ever missed a day of riding. He rode exactly nine miles every day, he informed me, taking the same route every time. Given the small acreage and limited number of streets in Spring Hill, I can only imagine how boring and monotonous his rides must have been. He never rushed or seemed to vary his speed, and I'd guess he cruised along at five or six miles per hour. I'm thinking Don dealt with the monotony with frequent stops to talk with neighbors who were outside doing other things, like walking their dogs, going to the mailboxes, or gardening in their front yards. He even stopped to talk to us sometimes, which is how I got to know him.

After over four months of bicycle ownership and riding, I'd decided my riding fell about halfway between how this elite-looking cyclist rode and how Don rode. I loved speed and tried to maintain a cruising speed between nine and eleven miles per hour. I had ridden faster in my forties and fifties, of course, but at seventy-five I was pleased to do as well as I did. I'd never have been able to keep up with the long, tall speed-loving neighbor. I gloated at the thought, however, that I could leave Don in a cloud of dust. But then, perhaps I couldn't have. He looked about ten years my junior.

Unlike Don but like the Lance Armstrong wannabe, I left the subdivision when I rode. I would never have been able to go in circles and make all the frequent turnarounds that riding in the park entailed. I went out on the main streets, which had wide dedicated bicycle lanes and rode until I reached a bicycle trail. I lived about half a mile from a path paralleling Interstate-5, and that trail reached the Willamette River to the south in Springfield in less than four miles. It was not my favorite path because of the noisy highway. If I headed west, I'd reach the northern-most entry point to the Riverbank Trail system in just over two miles. That was my preferred route despite the repaving construction detours that seemed to never end along this stretch.

In the beginning, I'd feel good about myself if I managed to pedal ten miles on an outing. My first training schedule was to ride every other day. I then increased the frequency to two days on and one day off, which meant I tried to ride five days a week, although the days changed. I gradually increased my mileage, especially after finding a 14-mile Riverbank Trail loop that I loved. I increased my daily mileage to twelve or fourteen miles.

I remember so well the olden days when Michael and I were avid riders. We subscribed to *Bicycling Magazine,* and I fantasized back then of being an elite cyclist in training. I practiced intervals, with timed bursts of speed and then a timed recovery period before repeating the pattern. Michael and I were both working fulltime back then, and the training routines we followed emphasized faster, shorter rides on Tuesdays, Wednesdays, and Thursdays and slower but much longer rides on the weekends. We rested and tried to recover on Mondays and Fridays.

It'd been almost three months since I'd toppled over on my bicycle, and the humiliating memory had almost faded. My stamina and skills were improving, and I was even beginning to think of the bicycle as an extension of myself, like the machine and I were one entity.

Bottom line: I thought I was absolutely on top of my game. Strong. Fast. Confident. Ready for any surprise or unexpected challenge that might appear on my horizon while riding my bicycle. I felt like an elite rider despite knowing full well the thought was laughably hysterical.

And then the wind was sucked out of my sails, and my sails sank to the ground in utter humiliation. I blame what happened partly on my neighbor Don, the one who rode nine miles daily in his banana-yellow jacket, come rain or come shine. Or rain or clouds or fog, which was more likely during the fall and winter months.

"Why do you think Don wears that yellow jacket every time he rides?" I asked my astute husband.

"You can't figure that out?" Michael's tone conveyed incredulousness. "He's wearing it for safety, so us old geezers won't run him over as we crawl along at five miles per hour."

"You think he's afraid one of his neighbors might hit him?" Michael rolled his eyes rather than bothering to answer.

I considered Michael's response. About a third of the folks in Spring Hill didn't drive anyway. I saw rideshare vans, younger folks, Ubers and cabs, all sorts of outside vehicles here taking residents hither and yon. Yet I'd watch Don laughingly ride his bike up on the sidewalk and stop on the other side of the street one time when I was backing out of my driveway. At the time, I hadn't thought it was very funny. He obviously did since he laughed and waved when I drove by.

But one had to be extremely careful backing out of garages and driveways in this community. Folks walked down sidewalks with 12-ft. leads on their dogs, stumbled along with canes and walkers, and occasionally tootled by in motorized wheelchairs. I'd learned to back up very slowly, looking in all directions multiple times as I eased out into the street from the garage.

The next day, over breakfast, I asked Michael, "Think I should get some kind of reflective vest or jacket to wear when I ride? I see a lot of folks on bikes wearing those green or yellow jackets, and they often have these huge blinking lights on both the fronts and the backs of their bikes."

"Of course. You should do all those things."

I went online to Amazon and ordered a bright yellow rain repellant jacket with reflective stripes. The more I thought about it, however, the more I didn't want to wait the two weeks Amazon said it would take for delivery. I cancelled the order and raced over to REI that very afternoon. I came home with exactly what I wanted, and it had even been on sale.

The next morning, I felt very self-righteous as I donned my new jacket. I already had lights on my bike but didn't always turn them on. That day I did, feeling invincible as I took off for my daily ride.

At my first stop, where I had to push a button to turn on flashing lights to alert motorists that a pedestrian was crossing the street, the hem of my new jacket caught on my bicycle seat as I dismounted to push the button. It was like a slow-motion debacle. I saw it, I felt it, but I was helpless to circumvent the tumble that took place. I couldn't friggin' believe I'd fallen for the THIRD time on this bicycle.

Once again, the only thing that seemed wounded was my foolish pride. I found a skinned knee later when I switched from my riding tights to jeans. I couldn't believe I again dodged a bullet and escaped with no bleeding wounds or broken bones.

I'd gotten a little dirt smudge on my new jacket when I fell but managed to scrape it off with my thumbnail. I still had the tags and the receipt, so I'd take it back to REI and cry if necessary to get them to accept a return of this used item. Surely, they'd have compassion for a sweet little old seventy-five-year-old woman who could end up permanently disabled from wearing an unsafe REI jacket, right? I thought I could make a good case.

I had to seriously wonder if I'd lost my mind though. Was it really a good idea for me to be out there, trying to live as if I were still fifty, riding a two-wheeler on slippery, leaf-covered trails, dodging homeless people, wheelchairs, walkers, dogs on long leashes, and babies in strollers, when I couldn't even manage to stay upright?

That third fall challenged any notions I might have had about being an elite cyclist. I was thankful it happened away from home and not seen by any of my neighbors, especially not that chick in the fancy kit.

CHAPTER 22

Guerrilla Gardening

Gardening is one of the most relaxing activities I've ever found. It's better than practicing Yoga, walking in the woods, or curling up under the covers on a cold, rainy afternoon with a good book. Since moving into Spring Hill, however, a gardening unease has evolved, creeping in almost imperceptibly. I realized my Oregon gardening, unlike decades of Florida playing-in-the-dirt bliss, left me a bit agitated and perturbed. I needed to figure out why.

How could a little manicured yard in an over-55, cookie-cutter community leave me wanting to dig in my heels and fight? I knew the answer: My yard didn't make me happy despite the exorbitant amount of money I'd spent on plants and hardscaping. Plus, where was that phenomenal growth my new neighbors had promised would occur here in the Willamette Valley? I planted things, and they seemed to just sit there and do nothing. Yes, I understood that initially plants needed to develop strong root systems before they started producing foliage and flowers, but neighbors had led me to believe all these plants I put in the ground would double or triple in size during their first year. If my new plants were doing anything at all, it was underground, which means I couldn't see it and was completely unimpressed.

I wanted a beautiful garden, not some half-hearted, mediocre version of what everybody else had. Yes, my competitiveness was obnoxious, but

I just couldn't shake it, not after some of the remarks that neighbors had made to me. Like Sarah's admonition to forget about being a Master Gardener because nothing I knew would work here anyway. Or Mildred's speculation that my yard would be a jungle in a couple of years, and I'd be digging out half the stuff I was now planting. She thought I was planting things too close together, which I later realized I was. Or the neighbors who'd stop to look and ask questions but refused to comment, even when I fished for their opinions and advice. I had to up my game, and I needed Manny's help for my ideas to reach fruition. I simply no longer had the energy or the strength to do all this yard work by myself.

Manny's eyes widened in excitement when I shared my gardening vision with him. I imagined a backyard filled with patios, water features, and seating nooks. I wanted winding paths with lush hedges for privacy and smaller perennials for color, texture, and variety. A water-guzzling, eco-unfriendly lawn like the one I now had would not be part of the plan. I envisioned native plants flourishing with only occasional hand watering.

I could even see a small pond in my backyard oasis. This natural habitat would allow pollinators and wildlife to thrive. In terms of the wildlife, I already had bevies of birds at my backyard feeding station and a fair number of pollinators. Sometimes I'd leave a few unsalted roasted peanuts in the shell for the squirrels and could only shrug when I found they'd tried to hide them in some of the large container plantings on the back porch.

I had two small water features already—birdbaths made from gorgeous ceramic bowls snagged at my nearby thrift store with water wigglers sitting on top.

My next-door neighbor Mary Lou told me she had a birdbath and that crows would sometimes bathe and play in it. At first, this notion of crows throwing a party in my backyard horrified me. Who would want crows in their yards? But then I stumbled upon some fascinating information about crows, and I became a fan. I launched a mission to attract crows to my backyard by adding a large birdbath and trying to entice them with peanuts in the shell. After several months of ongoing efforts,

I'm sure my neighbors must have viewed me as a certifiable lunatic if they'd heard me cawing, calling, and sweet-talking a crow perched in a large tree several houses away. I didn't want to think about the opossums and rats my neighbors informed me also haunted my backyard while I slept. Bring on the crows. Although I haven't abandoned this crow-attracting mission, I've slowed down my flurry of efforts, since not a single crow has responded.

Manny initially looked bewildered by my backyard ideas—the ones about the hardscaping, water features, lush thick vegetation, and how it'd all combine into an ecofriendly wildlife habitat. I didn't share my crow vision with him.

"No grass?" he asked, and his voice began to fill with excitement. "I'll take it all out for you."

"For now, I only want the grass taken out from the porch to the end of the house, and I want a patio in the center with plants all around it."

"But I'll take out all the grass at once. It's easier that way."

"I can't tackle this entire backyard at one time. It's too much work."

Manny narrowed his eyes, lowered his head, and perhaps switched his ears to an off position. "I'll do the work for you, but all at once is the best way."

Manny obviously didn't understand, nor accept, that I couldn't deal with all the grass in my backyard being removed at the same time. He hadn't yet learned what a linear, sequential, obsessive planner and project undertaker he was dealing with. I politely said to him, "Best for me is one section at a time. I'm old, I'm new to gardening in Oregon, and I need to go slowly."

I wondered why I felt apologetic, or what made me feel I needed to explain my reasoning to my yard guy. I'd pay him to do the work, but I'd be damned if he'd make the decisions. It was my yard, after all.

"Hardscaping comes first anyway. Let's start with the patio. Here's sort of what I have in mind." I said it firmly, making it clear I wasn't going to change my mind.

My idea was a simple, inexpensive patio made of 12"x12" stepping stones, upon which I'd place outside furniture and several large containers of plants. Included in my vision was a raised cinderblock planter at the end of the new patio where I could grow green beans, squash, cucumbers, and maybe even a couple rows of corn.

Manny's mood lifted as we talked, and his eyes positively twinkled as he began talking about a large rotunda-shaped patio with varied earth-toned pavers. "I know the perfect one. Right here," he said as he began indicating the boundaries. "I will bring a flyer for you to choose the one you want. They're all from Lane Forest."

Lane Forest was a local wholesale and retail business that specialized in garden-related things, including patios, water features, and plants. I knew Manny had a business account with them and could buy at wholesale prices.

Three days later, Manny dropped off a Lane Forest rotunda patio flyer, which showed three different sizes, four different designs, and several earth-tone color options.

I looked at those patio photographs, fell in love, and wondered how I'd become such an easy mark. I'm not generally impulsive, but I could clearly see this beautiful round patio in my backyard. I already imagined sitting at my desk in the office and looking out at this beautifully land-scaped, color and texture-filled botanical wonder while I wrote. When the weather permitted, I could set up a small workstation on the porch for my laptop. Or better yet, I could sit under the umbrella at the table on my new patio and read a book while sipping a glass of cabernet. Yes, I could totally see this in my backyard.

Like me, Manny had a vision, and as I listened to him talk about "our" patio project, I came to appreciate his ideas and his eye for design. He wanted to bring in boulders as accents and granite for stepping stones. He marked off an area for a raised garden bed. As he left, he promised to work up a written estimate and get it to me within a few days.

Michael had been present for much of this patio discussion, and I was surprised to note that Manny seemed to be "pitching" more to Michael than he was to me. Manny's parting words, perhaps directed more at Michael than to me, were, "Now don't be shocked at the price. It'll be expensive but very beautiful."

I realized that Manny probably thought that Michael would give the final approval or disapproval for the project. Is the word 'rankled' a more intense description than the word 'bristled' when confronted with what I perceived as only thinly-veiled sexism?

It was expensive, but as the work progressed, I became more excited than ever about this patio project. Manny spent several days removing sod, leveling the ground, and filling in a gravel foundation. When he started installing the rotunda pavers, even Michael would walk out often to inspect the progress and nod his head in approval.

Manny's work at my house drew attention from the neighbors. To haul in supplies, he had to back his truck and trailer into my driveway and move material through the garage and across the porch to get to the construction site, thus leaving a clear view from the street and sidewalk straight through to my backyard.

Manny became my hero, and by mid-December, he had almost completed this beautiful addition to my backyard. *Almost* is the operative word in this story. But alas, winter arrived, and the weather turned nasty. Rain, sleet, and snow made the near-freezing temperatures even less tolerable, and Manny decided to wait for better weather before finishing the project.

While my eagerness to start putting in landscape plants nearly consumed me, I understood this was not the time of year or the kind of weather to expect plants to get off to good starts. Still, Manny could have finished the damn patio so I'd at least have something pretty to look at while waiting for spring.

The new year arrived, and the cold, rainy weather continued. Manny continued to focus on other projects in the neighborhood; it was as if he'd completely forgotten about my patio project. Over the winter, I learned that Manny did all sorts of other projects, such as cleaning gutters, pressure washing sidewalks and driveways, building raised garden beds, and laying in edgers around flowerbeds and along sidewalks in front yards. I took advantage of Manny's availability and hired him to string LED lights around my patio roof and along the side of the house where the beautiful new but still unfinished rotunda-shaped patio sat. I couldn't help but wonder, however, how finishing my patio didn't feel okay to Manny because of bad weather when he spent six or seven hours a day pressure washing my neighbors' driveways and sidewalks, leaving him soaking wet in the bitter cold.

Weeks turned into months. I'd walk around my neighborhood, hoping no one sensed I was scouting for Manny's truck. I wanted to see which resident he was working for that day, which neighbor he was prioritizing over me and my patio project. He started big projects for some, and I'd see his truck for three or four consecutive days at the same house. Seldom could I figure out what the hell he was doing in those backyards, but obviously the projects meant more to him than mine. Why else wouldn't he just come and spend four hours finishing my damn rotunda patio? Chagrin turned to irritation and eventually mushroomed into anger. Was this dude jerking me around?

Had I somehow offended Manny that he had turned his back on me? Was he punishing me for an offense or some slight I wasn't aware of by leaving my patio unfinished? Initially, he'd been such an enthusiastic supporter of the project, raving about how beautiful the landscaping looked as I gradually added plants. He had invited passersby to come and inspect the project while he'd been constructing it. I would walk out to my backyard sometimes and be surprised to see someone from the other side of the development standing on my porch listening to Manny explain the vision. He told me he'd already picked up three new jobs after neighbors saw my in-process patio.

I revisited all the ways I might have offended him. Perhaps I'd talked too much to Carmen, making him feel that I'd disrespected his role as the boss and head of his household. Maybe he was angry because he'd told me he'd plant the area around the new patio, but I was doing it myself rather than waiting for him to get around to it. I hadn't been tipping him, but maybe I should have been? His charges were so outrageous, however, that I felt like he'd included the tip already in the bill.

I stewed at the thought that he and all these other yard maintenance crews in this over-55 community might be taking advantage of us seniors, just because they could. Did all these guys get together and decide upon inflated rates to charge? Did they collectively collude to fleece us for more money than they'd ever be able to get in a "regular" neighborhood because of our physical limitations, medical diagnoses, trusting natures, or maybe even our poor memories and dwindling cognitions? Surely no one would take advantage of the elderly, I thought. Yeah, right.

The most infuriating aspect of my frustration was knowing I could not confront Manny directly with my anger. Reliable, competent gardeners were hard to come by, and I knew of at least one new neighbor (in Eleanor's old house next door to me) who'd spent three months trying to hire one of the existing lawn crews in Spring Hill without any luck. None of the companies were taking on new customers; they were all already overbooked. Plus, Manny had a reputation of being quick to anger. I'd heard the story of one hapless homeowner who'd confronted Manny about something he'd done, and Manny exploded and quit.

But the fear of losing Manny's services and not being able to find a replacement was not the reason I knew I'd never confront him. Rather, I knew I'd never find a more conscientious, fastidious, and perfectionistic landscaper. I knew he'd eventually finish my patio and that it would be beautiful and perfect. I needed to just simmer down.

Spring finally began to tease its arrival, and I combed garden shops with unbridled enthusiasm. I spent hours online, researching plants and what might thrive in my Zone 8b yard. I talked with neighbors about their plant choices, and I tried to identify every healthy, attractive plant in the subdivision, since at this point, I didn't really know what I liked or wanted.

Eventually I realized my anger at Manny stemmed from my neediness. As I began to gradually add preliminary plantings around the back porch and patio, I felt my seventy-something years in every muscle and joint in my arthritic body. It'd been years since I'd dug holes in a yard, and I'd never dug in rock-filled clay. After planting a couple of small plants in one-gallon containers, I'd find myself exhausted for the rest of the day.

I looked around my almost-barren backyard in dismay. It was too big and too empty. The thought of all the holes I'd have to dig to fill it with plants overwhelmed and depressed me. I'd never be able to landscape this yard by myself, as I'd always done in the past. I needed Manny's brawn, and I'd have to accept his timeline and pay him dearly for his services.

But my sorrow went even deeper than that. Even if my plants thrived in the Willamette Valley, and even if they tripled in size each year, I'd never live long enough to see my vision materialize. I'd never see every slat of my white vinyl fence hidden behind hedges three feet higher than my fence or the cracks in my steppingstone paths filled with moss.

I wasn't angry with Manny. I was angry because I knew I would die long before I was ready. Metaphorically, I was probably digging my own grave as I dug holes for my new plants.

My only consolation was that one day I'd perhaps be able to befriend a few crows who'd talk to me, bring me shiny presents, and maybe even perch on my hand or shoulder.

CHAPTER 23

Black Widows Weave Webs

Unexpectedly, Shelley sent me a message on Facebook. "Come to Mac's Saturday night and bring that guy Jeremy with you." She went on to describe a wonderful blues band from Portland that'd be playing an outside concert on the lawn.

"Are you friggin' kidding me?" I asked Michael after reading Shelley's message. "You think she really likes Jeremy or is she just messing with me?"

Michael shook his head. "I think she just meant that she'd like us to join her and that it'd be fine if he came, too," he said. "What a nice note. We gonna do it?"

Not sure how I'd become the scheduler, i.e. social planner, in the family, but it wasn't a job I'd ever wanted. I couldn't help but think that probably Norma Jean had been Jeremy's scheduler.

"Let's not decide now. It's supposed to be a hundred degrees tomorrow. I don't want to sit outside on the lawn in that kind of heat."

Later, when I told Jeremy that Shelley wanted to see him at Mac's Saturday night, his response stunned me. "Well, I may have a date that night, so I'll have to wait before letting you know."

I was glad we were texting so he couldn't see my shock. "Who's the lucky woman?" I blithely texted back, hoping he didn't think I was being inappropriately nosey.

"It's someone I met online on Facebook. She lives in Springfield. I'll keep you posted."

Later in the afternoon, I texted my friend Maggie that Shelley had asked about Jeremy and wanted to see him. Maggie's response was: "Tell him to be very careful."

While I don't want to sound catty, I had to chuckle. I didn't need Maggie's input on Shelley's potential to hurt Jeremy. Shelley could chew Jeremy up like a woodchipper and turn him into mulch in seconds flat if she chose to do so.

The thought of me as an intermediary in someone's dating/mating affairs made me think of the mafia. I didn't want to get involved, lest anyone think I might warn anybody about anything. Shelley could probably pulverize me as easily as she could Jeremy. I liked my image as a sweet little old lady just fine. I wasn't going to deliver any messages to anybody, thank you very much.

That night at the wine bar, Jeremy and I had a chance to chat privately for a few minutes. "So, tell me about this date you've lined up for tomorrow night."

"She's a forty-year-old Hispanic woman, and she's absolutely gorgeous. We were first talking about meeting in the late afternoon for coffee, but then she said that maybe after coffee we could go for dinner. If we clicked, that is." He paused, shaking his head and sighing. "I'm thinking of suggesting we just skip the coffee and go straight for dinner. We'll work out the details in the morning."

I couldn't think of an appropriate response and wisely said nothing, hoping Jeremy would continue talking.

"Honestly, I keep asking myself why a beautiful woman like this would be interested in someone like me. I've already told her I don't give out money. She says people have tried to scam her, too, so I'm glad we got that out of the way before meeting in person. Still, she's got to be after something."

Another friend came over and plopped down in a chair next to us, ending our conversation.

Later, as we were all leaving the wine bar, our friend Linda turned to Jeremy and said, "I've got a friend I want you to meet. I've told her all about you, and she's interested."

Jeremy grinned. "Great. I'll look forward to that."

Jeremy called early Saturday morning to say his date with the gorgeous Hispanic woman had fallen through and he'd really like to go to Mac's that night to see Shelley. Being nosey, I couldn't help but ask what'd happened with his dinner date in Springfield.

"It got really bizarre," he said. "When we changed it to dinner rather than coffee, she started telling me what a great cook she was and how she'd like to make dinner for me at her house. But she got real squirrely when it came time to give me her address." He paused. "Something was really off about the entire thing. I finally realized she was probably a prostitute, and the free dinner might cost me a thousand bucks. I called her back and said to forget it."

"Wow. That's quite a story," Michael said. "She might have been concerned that you were a cop and would arrest her." Michael and I always turned our phones to speakers when we talked to Jeremy so we'd both be able to talk and hear the updates.

"Or maybe she was a cop setting up a sting and waiting for you to say the magic words and offer money," I said. "I think you dodged a bullet with this one."

"Yeah. I should have picked up that it was some kind of scam earlier than I did."

Oh Jeremy, you are so naïve and trusting. However, instead of voicing that thought, I went in another direction. "How are things going with your dating coach?"

"Really good." Jeremy explained that he'd just had his fourth of twelve sessions with the coach, and this time he had homework to complete. "He's taken some chart from business, and is applying it to dating, helping folks like me prioritize the characteristics that are most important in a partner. Before next time, I'm supposed to select twenty women and try to fit them into all these categories." He sounded excited about the assignment.

If Jeremy planned to have me as one of his twenty subjects, I hoped he wouldn't tell me how I'd ranked. Based on what I perceived as his priorities, he'd probably have me as number nineteen or twenty because I was so old and wrinkled.

"Can I ask how much this coaching dude is charging you?" I made my question sound as innocent and natural as possible, realizing it was none of my business.

"It's only $1,600 for twelve one-hour sessions." Quickly doing the math, I realized this guy was making about $135 an hour while sitting at home with quite probably no credentials and no oversight from anyone. Or maybe he had credentials. Maybe he'd been in the dating scene himself for years, trying out different pickup strategies and personas. Maybe he was still testing out various strategies to make people trust him enough to share their credit card numbers.

The next night, after stopping at two other venues before arriving at Mac's, the temperature had cooled to a tolerable level. Shelley spotted us, waving us to come sit at the table with her and a friend. As soon as Michael and I sat down, she grabbed Jeremy's arm. "You're coming with me," she said and led him off into the crowd.

"Guess that answers the question of Shelley's message on Thursday," I said to Michael. "She is interested in Jeremy, and that invitation to Mac's was for him, not us."

We hardly saw Jeremy for the rest of the evening. He danced to that Portland band even more than I did, sporting a huge grin that never left his face. On the way home, he excitedly told us Shelley had invited him to go up to Albany the next afternoon to sing karaoke, which was one of his favorite hobbies.

The next day, Jeremy made a Facebook location post showing that he was in Albany singing with Shelley at a karaoke event. When Maggie saw the post, she texted me: "You need to tell him about Black Widow Spiders. They devour their partners after mating. LOL"

🛺

Jeremy was one of the most tenderhearted, devoted, and loyal guys one could ever meet. He had stood by Norma Jean to the end, and he now clung to his two Chihuahuas, Ivy and Fern, in her absence. When

I asked the next day about his singing date with Shelley, he said she had asked him to return to Albany that night and join her at a jam.

An hour later, Jeremy texted to say he'd changed his mind about going to Albany. "I feel too guilty about leaving the dogs," he said. "It's just not fair to put them in a crate at 3:30 in the afternoon two days in a row." Instead, Jeremy talked us into going with him to a brewery hosting an open mic. I'm certain visions of stardom with his new singing partner, i.e. Shelley, flashed on his internal screen. At one point in the evening, he even said, "I could probably find a guitarist and sing in an open mic like this. Some of these folks aren't very good." My ears had already come to the same conclusion about most of the participants. However, I couldn't comment on my friend's talent since I'd never heard him sing.

As we sat listening to the good, the bad, and the downright ugly at that open mic, Jeremy shared a startling bit of information about our two blues bar women friends, Maggie and Shelley. "Shelley told me Maggie got really upset because I was spending time with her. Seems they had words over it, and Shelley has now Unfriended Maggie on Facebook." He turned to me and asked, "Do you have any idea what that's about?"

"Sounds like a cat fight, the kind teenaged girls get into." I didn't add that this story didn't ring true to me. I wanted to tell Jeremy I'd bet my house that Maggie wasn't jealous of Shelley, that she wasn't interested in him, and that she could care less if he liked Shelley. I could even have told him about Maggie's warning to be careful and later describing Shelley as a Black Widow. But those things sounded mean-spirited to say, so I kept my big mouth shut. But I nevertheless wondered if Maggie had now become Shelley's spidery prey, with Shelley devouring her electronically via Facebook excommunication. But that didn't ring true either. Eventually, I'd muster the courage to ask Maggie about this, since Maggie was my friend and I hardly knew Shelley, other than being Friends with her on Facebook.

However, Jeremy seemed to like Shelley, and I didn't want to pass judgment on his dating choices. I didn't know either of these women very well and would not have vouched for either, at this point. I regretted my texts to Maggie telling her about Jeremy's singing rendezvous with Shelley. I vowed at that moment to cease all communication with everyone except Michael when it came to Jeremy's social activities.

For someone who'd never wanted to get involved, I'd surely gotten myself in over my head. Now I wanted out. I didn't want to hear another story, no more updates or installments, and thank you very much but I'd like to focus on my own life from now on.

"Good luck, Little Gerri," my sarcastic hubby said when I vented my angst. "You're stuck in the Black Widow's web as much as anyone, and I'd bet you're not going to get untangled for a long, long time." Michael laughed. "But I believe you've got a Black Widower rather than a Black Widow." I didn't share my husband's amused analysis of the situation.

CHAPTER 24

Internal Politics

"We were full time RVers for seven years before settling down here," Harold told us. We met Harold, husband of Mildred from the Social Committee, the first time we attended a Saturday morning coffee at the clubhouse. "A lot of these folks RVed before moving in here," he added.

During that first clubhouse coffee, I had shared with Harold that I had written three books about RV travel, and he responded that he was a writer with several published books as well.

"What's your genre?" I asked.

"Oh, they're just technical books. I'm a physicist," Harold said. When I later looked up his books on Amazon, all seven of his books were about investment strategies and design. His author profile showed he was a Ph.D. with multiple advanced degrees in mathematics, physics, and investment engineering. He'd also held multiple university positions, including that of dean. I tried to read a few sample pages in one of his books on Amazon and confess that I had no idea what he was talking about. That insight gave me pause, thinking I might be grossly under-estimating the intelligence and achievements of some of my neighbors.

A short time later at Saturday coffee, as the thirty or so community residents were finishing up their pastries and coffee, Mildred got up to speak. She informed the group of several upcoming activities and a couple of "issues" of interest. A neighbor to the left of me at the table whispered that Mildred was chair of the Communications Committee and interacted with the owners and management of the park.

I'd later learn that the Communications Committee was *the* self-appointed governing board for the community. Not that the committee had any power, since the community's bylaws governed everything, and management controlled those bylaws. We'd later learn that some of those bylaws were archaic, especially when it came to landscape management.

"Maybe manufactured homes are the grownup version of RVs," Michael said with a chuckle as we walked back home. "This might be where old RVers come to die."

"Not funny. I don't even want to think about that." I could easily see the logic of the transition though. Folks here owned their homes but rented the land, just as RVers did. That their homes now had no wheels didn't seem particularly relevant. Plus, these manufactured homes had a tight efficient design that felt like an oversized recreational vehicle.

"Harold and Mildred certainly seem to run this neighborhood, "I said. "Their status seems firmly cemented. It's like folks grovel over them."

"They seem to be the kingpins, that's for sure."

I'd later learn that my friend Mary's husband was also a retired university professor, having taught sociology at a major university in the Midwest for decades. Another neighbor, also male, had been the Eugene Police Chief for twenty-five years before he retired. I realized many other highly educated and accomplished folks probably lived in this neighborhood. I hoped that some of them were women, and that eventually, I'd get to meet them. As most of the women I'd met so far were in their late sixties and older, I realized that most of them probably grew up with the same limited options in terms of careers as I had. It dawned on me that my bitter reaction to that historical truth did not seem to characterize most of my contemporaries, leaving me to wonder if perhaps there was something wrong with me.

We gradually began to meet other ex-RVers, some of who still headed south for several months during the winter and stayed in Eugene the rest of the year. Our neighbors across the street did this and, in fact, had left a couple of months after we moved in. We'd never even gotten the chance to learn their names before they went poof for six months. They no longer RVed, however, and now owned manufactured homes both here and in Surprise, Arizona.

The weeks and months went by, and we continued in our failure to find any gravity with folks in our neighborhood. Michael went four or five times per week to the exercise room in the clubhouse, which he came to think of as his private gym since there was never anyone in it. He liked to tell people, "I can go in on Monday and then again on Wednesday, and absolutely nothing will have changed. Why wouldn't I call that room mine?"

Before buying my bicycle, I walked for exercise. I'd usually choose walking around the neighborhood in circles rather than taking the long stretches on sidewalks outside the park. I felt desperate to make connections and made it a point to stop and say hello to anyone I saw outside, whether they were walking, gardening, getting their mail, or doing something else. After a while, it began to feel like my neighbors were humoring me. They'd stop whatever they were doing, politely answer any questions I might ask, and shuffle their feet with impatience to get along on their way to whatever they'd been doing before I interrupted them and started yakking. They rarely showed any interest in me.

One time, during the rotunda patio installation project, our bicycling neighbor Don stopped to ask what we were building in the backyard, and we invited him through the garage and onto the porch to see for himself. During our casual conversation, somehow the subject came up of how Michael and I were finding it difficult to get to know people in the neighborhood, sharing that in our previous community neighbors would drop in, sit on the lanai, and have a beer or a glass of wine while visiting for a few minutes. Our neighbor Don informed us that he and his wife simply never went into other people's homes and never invited folks into theirs. "It just isn't done around here," he said, giving us a look that suggested he thought we might be from another planet.

"You mean if we invited you over for dinner one night, you'd say no?" Michael asked.

"Yep. Chatting with folks outside for a few minutes is about as friendly as we'd ever want to get with anyone." He left shortly afterwards. Michael and I just looked at each other, not knowing what to say.

We grew to understand that this neighbor's attitude was somewhat typical. Standing in line at the grocery store, I'd find it easy to strike up conversations with strangers while waiting my turn to check out. We'd chat, sharing tidbits about ourselves and maybe even a few laughs to pass the time. After checking out, however, that friendly, vivacious woman, the one whom I'd have loved to nurture into becoming my best friend forever, wouldn't even bother to turn around and smile a goodbye as she wheeled her groceries out the door.

As I related stories like this to one of our Eugene friends, she shrugged and said, "That's Oregon for you. People come here to get away; they want to be left alone. They're friendly enough but usually don't want to get close. Look how many small towns and rural backwoods areas there are in this State. People don't want to live on top of each other. They want space, privacy, and quiet. We look at the east coast and freak out. How can people live scrunched up together like that?"

After living full time in an RV for almost three years, living in a single family home on a decent sized lot didn't feel at all scrunched up to me. Also, after living in an RV amongst strangers in RV parks for almost three years, I was tired of my privacy and all its ensuing quietness. I was ready to yak it up, hug, and make connections with other people. It was disappointing that the only places we'd been able to do this seemed to be our nearby wine bar and the old blues bar downtown. Folks took "the privacy of their home" to a level around here that I didn't understand.

"Nothing wrong with meeting folks in bars," Michael said. "No one seems to have let alcohol interfere with their lives, and it does raise the decibels on fun, in my opinion."

"Yeah, but you realize that all this drinking is going to eventually catch up with us, don't you think?"

"What do you mean?"

"Our bodies are going to betray us, Michael. Do you realize how many folks I've mentioned coming over one afternoon for a glass of wine here in Spring Hill, and how many of those people responded by saying, 'Well, I'd love to come over, but it couldn't be for wine. My body said 'no' to that years ago'?" I shook my head. "Seems that after a certain age, it interferes with sleep, it upsets the digestive system, it does this or does that. I cringe to think that's going to happen to me one day."

Michael snorted. "All the more reason to get it while we still can. Want to go to Oakshire Brewery for a little happy hour this afternoon? You're the one who's always quoting Janis Joplin."

What could I say other than 'sure'? I felt relatively safe to continue drinking. After all, my primary care physician monitored my kidney and liver functioning with annual blood work, and so far, cross my fingers and hope to die, my Salty Dogs and pinot noirs were not doing any observable, measurable damage to my internal organs. As much as I loved cabernet sauvignon, red grapes grown in the Willamette Valley were turned most often into pinot noirs, and I'd vowed to support local businesses to every extent possible.

The longer we lived here in Eugene, the more I recognized this ongoing, looping internal political tape that ran nonstop in my head. Things here felt strange and unfamiliar. This sparsely populated Pacific Northwest wonderland was as different than my previous East Coast zeitgeist as anything I could imagine. Sometimes I felt like an alien on another planet.

I felt blindsided by assaults and challenges from multiple directions. Our ages and declining bodies were major whammies that alone might have brought me to my knees. But I was now beset with the multiple closeup views into issues that I'd never seen firsthand: adjusting to the death of a spouse, older people trying to forge intimate emotional connections, meeting people and making friends in a new city where we hadn't known a soul when we settled here, watching our neighbors move in and out of the community as if they were playing musical chairs, seeing first responders on our street on a regular basis and gurneys with patients strapped down as an everyday occurrence, and perhaps the most scary of all, seeing unwelcomed changes in my husband and being certain he was seeing the same in me.

CHAPTER 25

On Not Being a Wuss

"Jeez," I wailed. "I'm not doing it." The afternoon was a gray, overcast forty-one degrees, and Michael had just suggested I should go for a bicycle ride.

"It's beautiful out there," he said. "Why wouldn't you go?"

"Because it's too cold." I'd bought my bicycle back in July and had gradually developed enough stamina to ride seventy-five or eighty miles per week, which I didn't think was that bad for a seventy-five-year-old woman. But then I caught a cold, bronchitis settled in, and I did not ride for twenty-five days. When I magically recovered from bronchitis overnight and ventured back out on the bike, I'd lost significant ground. My thighs screamed in pain after the first seven or eight miles, and I was panting like a dog in summer by the time I got back home. Maybe I was too old for this sport, after all.

Our house was warm and cozy, and I was an hour away from finishing a fantastic novel. Why would I want to freeze to death out there on a bike trail? Michael's little workout regime was mostly down at the Spring Hill clubhouse's small exercise room, where it was a comfortable seventy degrees. Except for the very short walk to the clubhouse, he didn't risk freezing his butt off when he exercised.

I knew Michael was right though. If Oregon was my new home, then I'd better adjust to the long, wet, and cold winters. I'd often see folks wearing shorts and t-shirts in this weather, sometimes even in the rain. I needed to buck up. Maybe figuratively grow some hair on my chest.

I bundled up—a t-shirt, a sweater, a heavy sweatshirt, and a windbreaker. I pulled a stocking cap over my head, which made for a tight fit under the helmet, and I tugged gloves onto my nearly numb hands. That was the best I could do and only hoped it'd be enough.

I rode about five miles, my face stinging from the cold. I vowed to get thicker, fur-lined gloves, as the ones I wore felt as sheer as panty hose. Yikes. It's been decades since I thought of pantyhose, an old-fashioned item of clothing I'd not be caught dead in anymore. Sort of like girdles, slips, and garter belts. I wondered why I'd let my husband shame me into going out on such a cold day.

I crossed the Willamette River on the pedestrian bridge at the Valley River Center, stopping in the middle to look down at the raging waters that flowed angrily to the north and fed into the Columbia River at the Oregon and Washington border. When I reached the West Bank Trail, a miracle occurred. The sun burst through the clouds and bathed me in light, and a grin erupted on my face. I looked up to see almost a hundred black birds perched on the bare branches of a huge maple tree, and I looked down to see dozens of white geese rummaging in the leaves, looking for insects. I knew in that moment exactly what I was doing on that glorious bike trail, and I vowed to never resist taking to the streets just because of a little coolish weather.

I don't always feel so euphoric on the bike trail. Sometimes I felt uneasy, almost scared. A few days ago, I took off in thirty-seven-degree, foggy and overcast weather, and I rode five miles on the I-5 Bike Path until I reached the Willamette River and the Riverbank Trail System. As I approached the riverbank, I saw a large man on foot coming toward me, bundled up in what looked like several layers of clothing. My pulse rate increased, and my throat tightened. He and I would meet on the trail.

When I first started riding the extensive trail network in the Springfield/Eugene area, I felt uneasy riding past tents and campsites. They most often appeared inhabited with men, although it wasn't unusual to see couples that included a woman or two. Still, the men outnumbered the women at least twenty-five to one. Also, it was not unusual to meet lone males of all ages walking the trail in isolated wooded spots, beside riverbank areas with thickets so dense someone could easily hide behind the bushes and jump out and grab some hapless and probably helpless old biddy like me. Or trees large enough that a predator could hide behind a trunk, totally out of view, again lying in wait for an unsuspecting mark to come along.

As I increased the frequency of riding, I became a bit more relaxed, especially when I realized it was not the physically unkempt, unhoused conditions of many of the folks I'd pass that caused the unease. As I rode towards lone figures, I had realized I always relaxed when I registered that the person was a woman rather than a man. I also understood that men walking dogs didn't feel threatening in the same way as lone males without dogs. Where did this come from?

One of the joys of riding a bicycle for me is the mental detachment that happens as I whiz along, my mind clear and thoughts free-associating in my head. New writing ideas sometimes occur, or some previously unrecognized connection between thoughts made that before seemed unrelated. Not long after putting it together that men made me nervous, I remembered a bicycling incident from my childhood. It now made sense.

My mini anxiety attacks stemmed from a buried fear of men. I got a bicycle for Christmas when I was five. Determination characterized my personality even then, and with minimal help from my parents, I learned to ride in one day. We had a large front yard with an unpaved driveway. For the first week or so, my parents allowed me to only ride on the horseshoe-shaped driveway in front of our house.

Finally, my begging to ride on the paved county road in front of our house paid off. My parents explained in detail all the rules I had to follow and how far I could go in each direction, making me repeat the instructions many times before letting me ride on the paved road. There was little traffic, and almost every vehicle that passed belonged to a neighbor. Mom and Dad could keep an eye on me from the house and from the barn.

I grinned nonstop as I raced up and down the asphalt, unable at five to put into words that glorious feeling of freedom of being out in the world by myself. Going a quarter of a mile in each direction from our house felt like being all alone, a new experience for me. I don't think I'd ever been this far away from an adult in my life. I felt grown up, strong, confident.

I wasn't the only non-motorist on that road, however. A couple of weeks into my newly found freedom, I saw a neighbor, Mr. Williams, walking slowly along the road on his way to Lee, the small town two miles to the north. Mr. Williams was old, poor, and lived alone in a shack in a wooded area not too far off the paved road and not far from where my family lived. Mom and Dad had pointed out his house to me before, reporting that he had neither electricity nor indoor plumbing in his house. My parents didn't seem to know much about him other than that he lived like a hermit.

Mr. Williams motioned for me to stop. "What a pretty new bicycle you have. Did Santy Claus bring that to you?"

"Yes, sir." Back in the fifties in the rural South, parents taught their children to be polite and respectful when talking to adults. I was only five and had never talked to a stranger before.

"You sure did learn to ride it fast, didn't you? Was it hard to learn how?" Mr. Williams took a couple of steps closer to me, close enough that I could smell the chewing tobacco in his mouth and the stench of his filthy clothes.

"Not too hard." I stiffened, suddenly feeling scared.

"When you were learning how, did you ever fall and hurt yourself down there?" He reached over and touched me between the legs.

"No, sir." I wanted to lurch away but found myself paralyzed. Fear? Confusion? Revulsion? How's a five-year-old supposed to know what to do?

"Well, you be careful now," he said as he turned and walked away.

I didn't say 'yes, sir' or anything else as I watched him lumber down the road. Somehow, though, the joy of riding my bicycle that day was over. I turned back toward home and unfortunately had to ride past that old man to get there. I speeded up and never looked at him when I passed.

"See you later," he called.

I didn't answer.

When I got home, I grabbed a couple of my favorite books and crawled into bed. Mom knew something was wrong.

"What's the matter, Sweetheart?" She sat on the side of my bed and put her palm on my cheek.

"Nothing." I choked as tears filled my eyes. I sobbed, unable to stop. Mom gently took my book, rolled me over, and started rubbing my back.

"What happened, Honey? Why are you crying?" She knew I wasn't a cry-baby and usually only cried when I got a spanking or got really mad.

It took about thirty minutes, but eventually Mom coaxed the story from me of what that nasty Mr. Williams had said and done. I could feel her body tense as she listened to my shame and confusion. Even then I felt that somehow it was my fault and that I had done something wrong. "It's okay now. That horrible man will never get near you again, I promise." I'd never heard her voice quite so strained. "Let's go to the kitchen and I'll make you some popcorn. That'll make you feel better."

Once I'd finished my snack and settled in with my paper dolls for the afternoon, Mom went out looking for my dad. We were a farm family, so both parents worked at home. My older brother was in school, and the school bus would be dropping him off soon. I somehow knew Mom wanted to tell Daddy what had happened to me before my brother got home.

I was quite a skilled five-year-old when it came to eavesdropping, and the dilemma my parents faced took several days before they finally settled on how to handle the situation. Mom wanted to call the sheriff and report the incident, but Daddy thought it'd be better to keep law enforcement out of it lest the neighbors found out and focused unwanted attention on the family. Instead of reporting it, my dad wanted to go talk to Mr. Williams and warn him to stay away from me or he'd end up in prison.

I overheard this prison tidbit one night when I was supposed to be sleeping, and I panicked. My knowledge of prison went only so far as the chain gang from a Georgia State Prison about forty miles away that mowed and cleaned the sides of our road several times a year. Eight or ten prisoners, dressed in black and white striped uniforms, would arrive in a big, armored van, accompanied by several armed guards. The guards would sit in the shade of either the van or a nearby tree, holding their big rifles pointed into the air and smoking cigarettes while the prisoners worked. In my five-year-old mind, if Mr. Williams went to prison, he'd be right back there on the road in the chain gang in front of our house several times a year. I'd never be able to ride my bicycle there again because he'd find me and keep touching me.

In time, I simmered down and again rode my bike back and forth on our paved road with unbridled abandon. I was vigilant to stay within the parameters my parents had set up since I didn't want to have them take my bike away for not following the rules.

I never saw Mr. Williams walking down our road again. Not ever. Did he find another way to get to town? I never found out. In time, I stopped thinking about what had happened, putting Mr. Williams's inappropriate touch way back in the recesses of my mind. Despite being a social worker, I personally had little patience for folks who built adult identities around childhood victimization. If anyone had ever asked, I'd have vehemently denied any emotional damage from the incident. As far as I was concerned, it was a nonissue.

And it remained a nonissue for seventy years, right up until I bought a bicycle and started riding the bike trail along the Willamette River in Eugene. That frigid morning as I zipped along on my bike on a nearly abandoned trail headed towards the Willamette River in Springfield, almost giddy on adrenaline and endorphins, that old man who lumbered along on that cold day reminded me of Mr. Williams in North Florida who had fondled me when I was five years old. I even caught an unpleasant, unclean scent from him as I whizzed by. The only thing missing seemed to be the plug of tobacco in his jaw.

I wish I could rid myself of this revived memory. Mr. Williams is long gone, and if I'd needed a victimhood status, I'm sure I'd have conjured one years ago. Still, I'm glad to know the origin of my irrational reactions on the bike trail toward the homeless camps, and I'm working hard to correct my now-dysfunctional responses to a seventy-year-old childhood incident.

I remember well in social work graduate school when readings and discussions focused on childhood traumas. I'd always viewed myself as resilient, with few if any lingering effects of that early sexual molestation.

However, while not revisiting the incident itself, I'd often second-guessed the way my parents had handled the situation. I resented my dad for being more concerned about protecting the family's privacy than protecting some other child from possible abuse by Mr. Williams. But mostly, I hated that my dad controlled almost every decision made in the family and, more often than not, ignored input from my mother. But even more confusing and upsetting, I couldn't shake my anger toward my mother for not being strong enough to overrule my dad. This was an irrational reaction and a quintessential example of blaming the victim, which my rational self understood completely. I was powerless to make it feel true emotionally.

As I grow older, I'm finding more and more memories popping up from the past, often out of nowhere with no discernable trigger. I'm trying to decide whether this is a welcome change that's coming as I near the finish line, or whether I'd be happier leaving these memories hidden and buried.

I'm more comfortable on the bike trail now. And I've made progress in acknowledging any discomfort and then letting it go. Objectively I understand and appreciate that the trail is there for everyone and that the unhoused have as much right to be there as I do. My unease seems silly and unwarranted. I'd never heard of any incidents on the trail of harassment or harm to anyone, although it was easy to speculate that such incidents might go unreported to the media lest widespread hysteria and panic erupt.

On Not Being a Wuss

My sister-in-law Carol raised the issue when she visited us. "Don't you get nervous out there on the trail by yourself? I've read that most of the homeless are either mentally ill or strung out on drugs."

"Don't be ridiculous," Michael said. "People just love to be afraid of the homeless. But you know what? Those guys don't want to draw attention to themselves. It's sort of like a brotherhood among them. If they start attacking and harming people, the city will crack down on them camping in public places. They police themselves as a way of protecting their right to squat on public land."

Carol and I looked at each other, perhaps both wondering where Michael came up with this explanation. It didn't make any sense to me, and I had no idea whether it made any sense to my sister-in-law. But in that moment, I also realized that a man would likely never truly understand how or why a woman might be afraid of men.

I recently read a newly released homeless statistic in *The New York Times*. The new information showed that per capita, Eugene, Oregon, had the highest ratio of homeless people in the entire United States, with New York City ranking number two. Michael and I had run into several native Oregonians who swore that both Texas and Florida loaded their homeless residents onto Greyhound busses with tickets to Oregon, usually Portland. Maybe the bus fares to Eugene were lower enough that this was now the destination rather than our beleaguered city to the north.

I'm embarrassed that I complained about riding my bicycle in freezing temperatures. Those poor unhoused people who lived in tents along the river were braver and hardier than I. Shame on me for being afraid of the victims, and shame on me for being such a wuss.

CHAPTER 26
The Contentious Garden Club

You'd think a topic as pure and innocent as gardening wouldn't trigger controversy and hurt feelings, right? The first time I attended the garden club meeting in Spring Hill, that illusion shattered. I made the mistake of revealing that I'd been a Master Gardener in Florida, and Sarah, the group leader, promptly informed me that my history as a Master Gardener in Florida meant zilch here in Oregon. I bristled inwardly, determined not to show my offense at what I considered a caddy remark.

Sarah was soon gone, however, and Jenny took her place. I soon realized Jenny was almost as outspoken as Sarah had been. In fact, I soon found myself feeling very bad that Sarah had broken her leg and ended up with a surgical wound that wouldn't heal, resulting in a relocation for her to assisted living. Sarah had at least smiled occasionally, which Jenny did not ever seem to do. (I later learned that Jenny lived in chronic pain, so apologies for my incorrect first assumption. In time, I'd learn that many of my early assessments were not always on the mark. Imagine that.)

One of my early garden club questions, perhaps more of an observation than a question, had to do with the almost nonstop running of inground sprinkler systems during the summer, the time when grass in Oregon should be dormant. The rainy season in the Pacific Northwest, for God's sake, is in the winter. I marveled at how lush and green my lawn stayed all winter long. In Florida, grass turned brown at the first hint of frost and didn't turn green again until April or so, when spring showers began to appear. "It's so wasteful of water," I'd said at one of the earlier garden club meetings.

"But our bylaws say there must be green grass in the front yards year-round," Jenny said.

"I'd really like to take out every blade of grass in my yard," I said, sort of knowing I should shut my mouth but somehow not doing it. "That's what I did with my Florida yard, converted it to xeriscaping. It was great—all those native, disease-resistant, drought-tolerant plants. During the worst of the hot, dry spells, I'd hand-water a couple of hours a week. Michael used to make fun of me, standing out there with a garden hose, but I used to love doing that."

"Nope, you're not going to get rid of your grass here," Jenny said, with what looked like a smirk.

"Oh, but you can," Angela piped up. "The bylaws just say your front yard must be green. I'm planning to have all my grass removed, and I'm going to fill the front and back yards with clover. It hardly needs water at all."

"You can't do that." Jenny snarled her response to Angela. "The bylaws say we have to have a green lawn, and clover is not a lawn."

I thought Angela would jump across the tables and strangle Jenny. "It says lawn, for God's sake. It doesn't say grass. A lawn can be anything green that's kept at a low height."

"Don't even try it," Jenny said. "Our corporation will never stand for it."

"But what about Lou Ann's artificial turf?" Someone else jumped in. "Her front yard is beautiful year-round, and from the street, you don't even know it's fake."

"And from the street, I don't think anyone sitting at this table will ever know my 'lawn'" (and she held up four fingers in the proverbial quotation marks indicator) "is clover," Angela said through clenched teeth, her voice tight and her eyes locked with Jenny's. "Besides which, I think in today's world, with water being such a precious and finite resource, I could probably take my front yard filled with clover all the way to the State Supreme Court and win my case."

I silently cheered Angela on, agreeing with every word she said.

Thus was my early introduction to the neighborhood garden club meetings. In retrospect, I wondered if I had triggered that kind of intense animosity or whether it'd been brewing indefinitely. I vowed at that moment to keep my friggin' mouth closed at future meetings.

Angela's sensitivity to environmental issues didn't always sit well with her neighbors. At the next garden club meeting, folks started talking about various potting soils and which stores in town had the best deals. A lot of residents in the park, I gathered, had large indoor houseplant collections. I perked up, interested in hearing what folks would say. I hadn't yet started a houseplant collection, but I'd been thinking about it.

Berta, the current president of the prestigious Communications Committee in Spring Hill Park, reported that she had found potting soil containing peat moss at half price at the nearby Bi-Mart. "I stocked up and bought four bags."

"You need to just throw that in the garbage can," Angela said, in such a dramatic tone I half expected her to jump across the table. "Don't you know that peat is an unsustainable resource? We're using it all up, and now they're saying we shouldn't use it at all."

The room was so quiet I could almost hear my own heart beating. Berta looked at Angela, her expression indecipherable, at least by me. While the silence in the room felt interminable, I'm thinking it ended after a few seconds when someone quickly changed the subject.

A couple of months later, I ran into Berta at the mailboxes one afternoon. "Where have you been, Berta? I haven't seen you at the garden club lately," I said.

"And you probably won't," she said. "I went to the meetings because there's so much I don't know about the plants in my yard, and I really want to do a better job. But I'll be damned if I'll sit in a meeting where some self-righteous bitch tells me I should throw away four unopened bags of perfectly good potting soil."

So much for the garden club being a conflict-free zone. Or for a common love of plants to overshadow any minor differences of opinion related to gardening practices.

One of the most beautiful yards in Spring Hill belonged to a former site manager of the park, Matt, who lived across the street from Michael and me. Matt had bought a home in this community when it opened in 1998. He appeared to be well into his eighties, though he is still agile enough to climb ladders with his chain saw to trim large trees every year. I've never seen his backyard, but it sounds as if he has planted every square inch with edibles—artichokes, blueberries, and every summer vegetable imaginable. His wife Lynn grows roses, and Matt often mentions at garden club meetings that she keeps fresh flowers in the house nonstop during the spring and summer when her roses are in bloom.

Matt voices high respect for the Master Gardeners, sharing with me that he'd completed the entire, lengthy, laborious training through the Extension Service. He still has and uses several thick loose-leaf binders of educational material he'd received as part of the program, voicing great regard for research-based gardening information. My kind of guy, for sure.

What sets Matt apart from many garden club attendees, and from the Master Gardeners I knew in Florida, is his warm embrace of multiple chemicals, including the much maligned and now off-the-market Round-Up, found to have caused cancer in throngs of users. Matt also reaches for nonorganic insecticides, fungicides, and other products to control diseases and pests. I think if the Master Gardeners ever caught wind of one of their former students using such toxic materials, they'd petition to have the name of their international educational program changed.

Sometimes I sense that Matt is politely taunting Angela when he only thinly masks a gloating smile while reporting how healthy everything is in his impeccable garden. He invariably begins his reports with a spoiler alert such as, "Now I know that some of you are not going to appreciate what I'm about to say, but . . ." And then, he proudly reports the non-organic chemicals he's used during the past month, including Miracle Grow.

"Oh, haven't you read about how Miracle Grow is killing all the pollinators?" Angela asked Matt, her eyes wide in alarm. "I used to use it on everything in my yard, but no more. And I don't think anyone else should be using it anymore either. What will happen to the world and our food supply when all the bees and butterflies and other pollinators have all been killed off?"

I suspected Angela must have been quite a drama queen in her earlier years, although she seemed to be maintaining her niche just fine now that she is in her mid-eighties. Somewhat like my ninety-four-year-old buddy Winifred who lives across the street, Angela looks like she'll be one of these folks who'll live forever, probably to the chagrin of residents who come to the garden club meetings specifically to hear about chemicals and nonorganic solutions that actually solve their gardening problems. I'm certainly not an advocate for toxic chemicals that poison the earth, but I do reach for slug bait and an occasional other inorganic solution for the hardy PNW slugs and other predators that thrive in my yard. Still, I admire Angela's spunk and the depth of her convictions.

Matt always seemed to welcome Angela's challenges. Perhaps they reminded him of his lengthy career as an attorney in the public housing sector where he challenged and argued points of law in enforcing housing standards. Angela's reactions suggested to me she felt Matt deliberately goaded her, and it did not please her one bit. I felt caught in the crossfire, for I liked and respected both Angela and Matt.

I found Angela to be one of the more interesting and likeable of the Spring Hill denizens despite her intensity and quickness to impose her ever-changing gardening beliefs and practices on others. I was very touched when she insisted on loaning me her favorite gardening book of all times, *Through the Season with Dulcy: More Favorite Columns by The Oregonian Garden Writer Dulcy Mahar*. It was a 2014 collection of newspaper gardening articles assembled and published by her son shortly after her death.

Per Angela, "My husband had been the gardener in the family, and he never wanted me to do anything in the yard." She pulled out her cell phone to show me photos of their one acre, lushly landscaped lot in South Eugene where they'd lived until her husband's death more than ten years earlier. "When he passed away, I knew I couldn't maintain that yard by myself, so I sold the house and moved here. And I decided that I'd become a gardener."

"You've certainly done a beautiful job with your yard," I said. We were standing on the sidewalk in front of my house, and Angela had stopped to chat. She showed a lot of interest in the plants I'd selected and the changes I'd made in my front yard.

"Yeah, I decided I wanted a classic cottage garden look in my front yard," she said. "I can't tell you how many months of reading and research I did in planning and getting this yard together. Now that I've got it just the way I want it, I think I can finally sit back and just maintain it, which'll be so much easier than planting it had been. I feel like I'm home free."

Imagine my surprise when less than two months later, at one of our monthly garden club meetings, Angela announced to the group, so much sadness in her voice I worried that she'd start crying, "Guess I'm going to have to redo my entire front yard. The summer was just too hot, and none of my plants are doing well in this heat. It's this global warming—time to switch to a different kind of gardening." She paused, dramatically as if to remind her fellow gardeners of the rightness and truth in her perceptions. "Be prepared to see clover in my front yard instead of grass that needs to be irrigated five times a week during the summer." She glared at Jenny while saying this.

"By the way," Angela shared with me during another front yard sidewalk chat, "I still use Miracle Grow on all my shrubs and trees. Once a month I attach the Miracle Grow bottles on the sprayer and give everything a good dose. I just don't use it on the annuals and perennials, the things I grow for the pollinators."

A few decades ago, I might have been outraged at the compromised integrity of my friend Angela, who obviously equivocated over what she considered the "environmentally correct" choices versus her awareness of what was effective. I had to wonder if maybe she didn't secretly use Round Up on her weeds.

Of all the garden club drama, the ongoing "issue" that might have moved me toward protest and action stemmed from a report from Mildred. Mildred was an active leader in the community and was not a woman anyone should challenge. In addition to being a birdwatcher and a steward of native Mason bees, Mildred was an avid food gardener who, like Matt, must have planted her entire backyard with fruits and vegetables. I'd probably never really know what was in Mildred's backyard, however, since in this neighborhood people didn't seem to ever go inside other people's homes or into their backyards.

At a garden club meeting in the fall, Mildred excitedly talked about the wildlife that came into her backyard. "In addition to all the birds, I also have raccoons and possums. They come, hoping to get some of the food I leave out for the feral cats." She paused. "I have a video camera with motion sensors set up in the backyard, so every morning Harold and I can see who came to visit." She grinned ear-to-ear.

"You feed feral cats?" Angela blurted out the question. I bit my tongue not to voice a similar shock and outrage at Mildred's revelation.

I noticed several people's eyes widen in surprise, which assured me I wasn't the only one who found feeding feral cats a questionable practice.

"Well, yes. They started showing up. There were four of them, and I knew they were after the birds that came to my feeders. I feed the cats so they won't eat my birds." Mildred reported this in the most matter of fact way possible, as if this logic made perfect sense.

"I have feral cats that come to my backyard, and I hate them." Angela said. "They potty, and it leaves a horrible stench, plus, they upset my dog. There are leash laws in this neighborhood, but people seem to think the laws are only for dogs."

"Why don't you call animal control and have the cats picked up?" somebody else asked.

"Oh, no," Mildred said. "I love cats. If I called animal control, they'd euthanize the poor souls. I could never do that."

"Well, I just hope your cats don't start coming into my yard," I blurted out, unable to control my shock. I, too, am a cat lover, but in my opinion, it was wrong to feed feral cats and thus allow them to propagate, spread disease, and use the nice, rich, fertile soil of gardeners like me as their litter boxes.

Someone in the meeting changed the subject, and I was glad. While I was horrified to learn Mildred was feeding these animals, I really didn't want to offend or upset any of my neighbors in this community. For better or for worse, I felt stuck here, and I'd promised myself that I'd try to make the best of it despite my mounting misgivings.

After the meeting ended, I walked back home on the sidewalk with Polly and another neighbor, expressing my horror over the feeding of strays. As I ranted, I noticed that neither Polly nor the other woman commented. Okay, you idiot. Keep your big mouth shut.

A few meetings later, Mildred again mentioned her feral cats, describing one as a Siamese mix with a white strip on his forehead.

"That cat comes to my backyard," Angela said. "It just sits and glares at me when I try to chase him away."

"All the cats are domesticated," Mildred said. "I think people have just dropped them off, or maybe folks in the apartments down the street just let them go when they moved away. I think they live in this little clump of bushes in the ten acres behind the park, facing Chad Drive. I think there's a colony of them that live together."

"Well, I certainly wish they'd stay out of my yard," Angela said. "There's another one, and this one is not feral, that belongs to a neighbor several houses down from mine. She leaves her garage door open about six inches so the cat can come and go during the day. It's against the park rules, and it makes me very mad."

At this point, Matt chimed in. "I happen to know it's against federal regulations for cats to roam free in any manufactured home community in this country." While he was obviously answering Angela, I noticed he looked directly at Mildred as he spoke. "I'm going to talk to the new park manager and ask her to enforce this law. I think the corporation needs to do something about this. Maybe I'll also write a letter to go in the monthly newsletter reminding people that there should be no cats roaming around outdoors unless they're on a leash."

While no one spoke, I sensed others sitting in the room sighing in relief, just as I did, that maybe someone could resolve this situation somewhere down the road. I managed to keep my mouth shut during this interchange, as did everyone else sitting around the table.

I feared for Matt, however. Mildred had a lot of influence in this community, and if she turned against him, it might make things a bit uncomfortable, at least in our little garden club.

With over a year's worth of garden club meetings now under my belt, I'd come to attend the gatherings as much for entertainment value as for gardening edification. Someone seems to utter some hapless little remark or comment at every meeting, and some other person leaves fuming over some perceived insult or another. Sometimes more than one. It's probably an indication of how my own aging world is shrinking that I would find amusement in this situation.

I also needed to consider, as I sat on my little self-appointed judgmental high horse, that I, too, might have invariably made critical and hurtful comments, totally oblivious to their reception and impact.

CHAPTER 27

Karaoke as a Chick Magnet

Jeremy was planning a cross-country RV trip with stops along the way to visit several adult children, stepchildren, and grandchildren. He wanted to drop by Mac's, the venue where he'd recently met Shelley, on his final night in Eugene. Michael and I were too exhausted from what had been three weeks of more partying and drinking than our old bodies appreciated, so we opted not to go to Mac's.

"We'd like to take you out for a farewell dinner," I said to Jeremy. "We'll go to a steakhouse at six or so. After we eat, you'll have plenty of time to swing by Mac's."

Over dinner, Jeremy mentioned that he believed Shelley was less interested in him than he was in her. At the same time, he said Shelley had talked of them possibly hooking up in New York in October, how they could pick up again when he moved to Eugene in the fall, and all the singing and music-related things they could do together. "But the bottom line for me," he said, "was that she was just too busy and unwilling to reschedule a single thing to fit me in again before I left. Sure, she'd have been happy if I'd driven up to Albany, but she wasn't willing to drive down here. That upset me."

I could understand his point. If he was interested in Shelley though, I couldn't help but think he drew a line in the sand awfully early in their relationship. They'd only had one date. Jeremy could be a stubborn man, and when he made up his mind about something, he paid little attention to new information. If I'd been Shelley, I might have been miffed at a guy demanding I drive down to see him in Eugene rather than him accepting that I'd had plans in place for weeks and therefore be willing to drive up to Albany. Still, I admired Jeremy for sticking to his principles.

Jeremy was a fast eater and finished his dinner before we did. We could tell he was getting antsy to get to Mac's. We shooed him on his way while we stayed for another drink. "You know he's planning to see Shelley tonight at Mac's, don't you?" Michael asked.

"He didn't say anything about it. I'd have thought he'd have told us if that was his plan."

"Just you wait and see."

I'm always surprised when Michael picks up on something I miss, but he was right about this.

"Shelley totally ignored me last night," he said the next morning in our farewell phone chat. "She was dancing with some guy. I know she saw me, but she never acknowledged my presence. I had one beer and left." Jeremy assured me he was fine and appreciated the clarification of where he stood with Shelley. "I'm just annoyed by all her mixed signals."

Michael and I have different interpretations of what had happened between Jeremy and Shelley. Michael thinks Jeremy was possibly reading things into Shelley's behavior that weren't there. I disagreed. I'd watched Shelley a couple of times with Jeremy, and I'd read her responses to his Facebook posts. In my opinion, she had led him on, and Jeremy had every right to feel miffed.

In retrospect, maybe I'd been wrong not to warn Jeremy of Shelley's Black Widow potential. At least she hadn't devoured him.

As he made his way across the country, Jeremy made almost daily Facebook posts about his everyday life. He posted the number of miles he rode each day on his bicycle, photos of dinners he cooked, oftentimes with the recipes, and reports and photographs of the karaoke equipment in his RV, to give a few examples.

The number of clicks and comments on Jeremy's Facebook posts from our friends in Eugene seemed to decline as time passed. However, after he began the karaoke posts, I noticed something that surprised me.

"Michael, remember how Shelley stopped commenting on any of Jeremy's Facebook posts after he didn't go up to that jam session in Albany?"

"Nope, I don't pay attention to things like that."

"I've been paying attention, and she dropped him like a burning ember. Until . . . listen to this. . . . He made that first post about practicing karaoke. Now, she's again commenting on all his posts, his song selections, and his attention to craft."

I'm left not knowing what to think about Jeremy's karaoke posts. Especially after my friend Maggie also started responding to his rehearsal posts, encouraging him on. I can only hope Maggie is not also a Black Widow, enticing her prey into her web as Shelley seems to also be doing.

Or maybe the two women, Shelley and Maggie, whom Jeremy believed were squabbling over him, were about to engage in a Facebook knockdown showdown. Perhaps karaoke was a disguised magnet for chicks. Who would have guessed?

Michael and I have not been able to reach the same page when we think of what little we knew of Jeremy's flurry of activities during those early days of seeking a partner. Our first-hand witnessing lasted only the three weeks Jeremy spent in Eugene, and even then, we knew there were things he didn't tell us.

Our points of agreement are of bewilderment and surprise. We'd both known people who'd lost spouses, but neither of us had ever had the kind of front row seat on older, retired people seeking partners. I'd certainly heard of online dating sites; my daughter had been active on a couple of them for years, but I hadn't understood how they worked and how predatory they seemed to be.

Michael and I shared a mutual concern that Jeremy was going to get conned, scammed, and ultimately damaged by some young slickster whose Tinder glamour shot photo he admired. It was unnerving to learn how easy it was for folks to develop an online identity and become anything and anybody they wanted to be. And I learned that many of those manipulators will latch right on to another's pain with their self-serving motives, and they'll do it in a heartbeat. Jeremy kept assuring us he could take care of himself, and while we knew he was a bright, competent man, we still worried because his pain and depression levels felt so overwhelming I feared they'd interfere with his judgment. I could not even imagine what he was going through.

Jeremy's situation made me wonder about the widowed women living in Spring Hill. Had they checked out online dating sites to find new partners after their spouses had passed away? Having been in my relationship with Michael since 1992, I was totally ignorant when it came to romance among senior citizens. It even crossed my mind that I, too, might have engaged the services of a professional to help me navigate the complicated and convoluted dating scene had I been in Jeremy's shoes.

I remembered a bit of street advice I'd received from singles when I first became a divorcee at age thirty-six. The happiest of remarriages reportedly came when widows and widowers connected. Widowed and divorced individuals usually didn't find that happy-ever-after that those who had lost spouses through death did. My sources seemed to believe that the "good catches" were snapped up within the first year or so. The longer one was single, the less the odds of landing in a successful second relationship. I divorced in 1984, and even then, research showed divorce rates among remarriages to be very high. Yes, this "M" word came with caveats lest one become too complacent about happy-ever-after endings.

Those common-sense speculations, all of which had a ring of truth in my mind, made me want to cross my fingers that Jeremy would soon find a nice widowed woman. Divorcees come with so much more baggage than widows and widowers.

When Jeremy pulled out of Eugene on his way east, his plan was to return to Eugene in several months and make this place his home. "Maybe he'll meet someone along his way to the east coast and fall in love," I said to Michael. "There's really nothing here for him to come back to, other than high hopes."

"And our friendship," Michael added.

In some ways, I felt grateful that Jeremy had given me a peek into what it might be like to lose a spouse and suddenly find yourself with the future you'd anticipated no longer there. I looked around Spring Hill at the widows I knew, though only casually, and wondered if their struggles to rebuild their lives as single women rather than as half a couple had been as difficult and painful as Jeremy's seemed to be.

Life in this over-55 community was opening my eyes to issues that I'd not previously considered. Given my age, the number of first responders in and out of the neighborhood, and the rapid turnover of houses as residents moved out to be closer to family, go into independent living or nursing home facilities, or simply because they passed away, I knew I needed to start preparing for my own future, which at my age would be for only a few more years.

And while that thought of only a decade at most of more life that'd likely be mine could potentially seem a rather depressing proposition, I embraced that epiphany in gratitude. I'd heard the wakeup call this time, and I needed to get my butt in gear.

CHAPTER 28
Just Say "No"

Shortly after we moved into Spring Hill, my neighbor Deidre recruited me to help with the monthly Saturday morning coffees in the clubhouse. Deidre organized this event and planned for the pastries and sweets. Volunteers made the coffee, heated water for the tea drinkers, and placed condiments on the tables. The hardest part, however, was the cleanup afterwards, including the rinsing and stuffing of the dishwasher with all the dirty coffee mugs, dishes, and silverware. Sometimes there'd be two or three loads of dishes before everything was clean and returned to their respective spots in the cabinets.

I agreed to help, figuring it'd be a good way to get to know my new neighbors. I sincerely thought at the time that volunteering would help me fit in.

Deidre bubbled with energy and enthusiasm, and she made me feel like I was her favorite person in the room. "Look at her go," Deidre said to all who would listen. "She's the most energetic, fastest-moving, hardest-working woman in this community."

While I would never have made claims like that about myself, I did notice that I probably did more work than any of the other volunteers. Not that this seemed to earn me any brownie points or even result in anyone other than Deidre and our next-door neighbor Mary Lou giving me the time of day during those coffee hours.

My zeal in showing up at these nine-thirty a.m. coffee hours waned, especially after I bought a bicycle and found mid-morning rides to fit into my Saturday schedule better than wasting two-and-a-half hours of time in clubhouse volunteerism with little penetration into the neighborhood cliques. Best friends scarfed up entire tables, and by the time the kitchen volunteers sat down to eat, Michael and I would end up sitting with the other misfits and outcasts. Not exactly what I'd had in mind when I told Deidre I'd be delighted to help.

A few days later, Mildred stopped me on the sidewalk coming home from the mailboxes. "How would you like to be on the Social Committee?" she asked. "It's just Mary Lou and me now, and we think you'd be a good fit. We're the ones who organize the monthly Friday night dinners in the clubhouse."

This invitation came about a month after I'd started helping with the monthly coffee gatherings and before I realized that volunteerism might not prove to be a quick path to making friends. My volunteered time and labor on the Social Committee moved me no further ahead socially than my time on the Saturday Morning Coffee efforts.

After a couple of months, I started "forgetting" the monthly Social Committee meetings, and then after joining the Hayworth Wine Bar, making friends, and realizing the wine bar had live music from six to eight on Friday nights, I began begging off helping at those monthly clubhouse dinners. Before I knew it, Mildred stopped reminding me of the monthly meetings, so I assumed I was no longer a member in good standing. Guess it didn't take a rocket scientist to figure that one out.

In retrospect, I didn't handle either of these committee involvements in the clubhouse well.

But what I finally began to realize was that I'd *never* been a good committee member for anything. My forty-year stint as a social worker had suited me to a tee, primarily because I had worked independently. Only periodically, maybe two or three times a month, did I have to work with other team members as we each shared our professional assessments for final treatment and educational planning.

And as I thought more about my difficulties in working with groups, I remembered those elementary school report cards—As and Bs for the academics, with Ss under all the social/emotional areas except for one. Under the category of "Gets along well in groups," teachers consistently awarded me Ns, which indicated that I needed to improve in that area. I was independent, and I liked to work at my own speed. Group projects and assignments tended to drive me crazy.

Coming from the large Tampa Bay Florida metropolitan area, home of three professional sports teams—Rays baseball, Buccaneers football, and the Lightning hockey—Michael and I were not prepared for the passionate ardor of the Eugene community over the University of Oregon Ducks. While support of the football team received the most enthusiastic support, the local loyalty extended to the university's basketball, volleyball, baseball, and track teams. To my amazement, the women's teams drew audiences almost as large as the men's, making me pleased even more that we'd settled down in Oregon. Not that college sports, or sports at any level, had ever captured and kept my interest.

But as I began to learn more about the Daisy Ducks and the extended Spring Hill coterie of Duck volunteers, I realized I'd missed a tremendous opportunity to join the socially elite of Spring Hill as well as the larger Eugene community.

The Daisy Ducks were a group of women volunteers who "served" the UO football team. Michael and I had never realized all the perks young athletes receive after signing contracts to play ball with a university. Mary Lou filled us in on what the Daisy Ducks did for the University of Oregon football players.

Nutrition was a major focus. The football team had its own chefs and dining hall. Team trainers carefully monitored every gram of food consumed by every player to ensure maximum variety and adequate intakes of the nutrients needed to build strength, stamina, and speed. For over ten years, Mildred and Mary Lou showed up every Friday at noon in the team's mess hall to help serve lunch. The large cadre of Daisy Ducks covered every meal seven days a week in the dining hall.

Mary Lou didn't tell us what Mildred's assignment had been, but Mary Lou's had been to serve the protein. Each player in line would present a card with his dietary regime to the server at each of the food stations. Mary Lou's job was to weigh the protein the player had selected, making sure the serving was exactly the amount recommended by the trainer. Mary Lou reported with a huge smile that she'd gotten to know every football player by first name.

"That's really interesting," Michael said. "You're no longer doing this?"

"We gave it up last year," Mary Lou said. "It got to be too much. Mildred is in her eighties now, and we'd end up standing there in the lines for at least two hours. She and I used to ride together, and when she stopped volunteering, I decided to stop, too. I didn't want to have to drive down there by myself each week."

"But there are other Daisy Ducks in this neighborhood, too, right?" I'd heard rumors there were but had no idea if it was true.

"Oh, yes," Mary Lou said with a smile. "There are nine of us here in Spring Hill. The others either cover the breakfasts, the dinners, or the Rice Krispie Treats."

"Rice Krispie Treats?" Michael blurted out his surprise.

Mary Lou laughed. "Yes, just like little children, those boys love Rice Krispie Treats. So, volunteers make up huge batches of them and serve them at halftime to all the players. It's a long-standing tradition, and I think the team would refuse to play the second half if the Rice Krispie Treats didn't show up."

While I found the Rice Krispie story interesting and surprising, the knowledge that there were nine Spring Hill women fawning over these overgrown boys fascinated me to no end.

Just think, I said to myself, if I had played my Social Committee card right, I might have become a part of this inner circle, and they might have let me measure out chunks of roast beef or make Rice Krispie treats, too. Oh, well. . . . Live and learn.

When we first moved into Spring Hill, I was surprised to see hand-written notices and announcements pinned to the community bulletin board that hung on the wall by the mailboxes. For big events, like the monthly coffees or dinners, organizers would make posters for a sandwich board display that would sit on the ground in front of the bulletin board.

"What's with this low-tech communication?" I asked Mildred one day. "Why don't folks use email or Facebook to communicate?"

"There aren't many people in this community who even know how to use computers," she said.

"I'd think Facebook would be a great way to share information, anything from upcoming activities to garden center sales to human interest posts about things going on in the neighborhood. For example, I'm new here and have no idea where to get a recycling bin for my yard waste. I'd ask that question on a neighborhood Facebook page, if there was one."

"The office manager can help you with the recycling bin, but the Communications Committee would be the place to ask your question about Facebook," Mildred said. "Down in the clubhouse on the little table next to the library, there's paper for people to write down suggestions and then a little box to put the suggestions in."

I went directly home and wrote out my reasons for thinking Facebook would be a great addition for the Spring Hill community. Two weeks later, I received a phone call from Berta, the chair of this powerful (sic) committee who said she thought my suggestion was brilliant and the committee had decided to create a private page for members of the park. Milton, a former resident manager with a long work history in IT, would be the Facebook Administrator and the committee thought I'd be an excellent co-administrator. Would I be willing to do this? Berta wanted to know. I accepted.

Before long, bulletin board notices went up and an article hit the press in Spring Hill's monthly newsletter presenting the creation of a private community Facebook group. Instructions were to email Milton, and he would accept folks into the group. I emailed Milton, and to my surprise, he waited a month before granting me admission into this private group, the one to which I was the co-administrator. I happened to know several people who contacted Milton after I did who he approved without any delay. So much for a shared responsibility.

The Spring Hill Facebook page did indeed get posts. I became Friends with half a dozen residents and began to feel a little more a part of the community. I used the page to pose gardening questions and occasionally to post a photograph of a plant that especially pleased me.

A year and a half after the page's creation, I was curious about the number of Spring Hill residents who'd joined the group. Although I don't have the total number of residents since it's constantly changing, a rough estimate based on a membership list showed that of the 102 homes in Spring Hill, fifty-six listed a single occupancy, forty-five listed a double occupancy, and one was listed as vacant. Therefore, the total population of the park, at that moment, was 146 residents.

It came as a shock to see the community's little Facebook page had a total of only thirty-eight members. I happened to know of at least six households in which both the husband and the wife were members, suggesting that out of 102 homes, the total Facebook membership represented only thirty-two homes, or thirty-one percent. Even fewer people than that ever participated by posting on the page. (I know of several members who have left the park, leaving me unclear as to how many new enrollees we might have. I know at least a couple of former residents who moved elsewhere but asked to stay on the Facebook page.)

I'd heard several people say they'd never join Facebook because of privacy issues. My friend Polly was one of those folks. I knew my next-door neighbor Mary Lou had joined the group, and she sometimes responded to posts I'd make. I don't think she'd ever made a post herself. Milton, my co-administrator, was the most active, with his posts generally about things going on in the neighborhood, such as garden shed break-ins and deadlines for paying the annual fees for yard waste removal.

To my amazement, Milton stopped me one day in the neighborhood Safeway and asked me if I'd be interested in taking over as the main administrator of the Spring Hill Facebook page. "I've just gotten too busy, and I'm trying to scale back on my activities," he said.

"I'll think about it and let you know," I said, hardly able to hide my shock. What I felt like doing was laughing. Milton had snubbed me so blatantly in the beginning of that Facebook page creation, and now he wanted my help? Unfortunately, my not-so-artful evasion of the question, combined with my convenient forgetting to get back to him, led to yet another ungracious handling of a situation. A few months later, I saw that my next-door neighbor Mary Lou was listed as the administrator of the Spring Hill Facebook page. However, when I subtly asked her about this one day, she had no idea what I was talking about.

Looking back, every single volunteer activity I'd undertaken in Spring Hill felt like a complete boondoggle. Or, it occurred to me, I was continuing to make no progress toward improving my deficient childhood social skills of being able to work well in groups.

A year after Milton first approached me to take over the private community Facebook page, he stopped me again, this time by the mailboxes rather than in the Safeway Supermarket to ask me again to be the Facebook Administrator. I thought about his request for a day, then impulsively emailed him and gave a resounding "Yes." What a perfect match for an asocial person like me. I'd be giving back to my community as a volunteer, but I'd be working independently at my own speed and at my own convenience. Yes, yes, yes. I'd finally found my niche in the Spring Hill Manufactured Home Park.

Maybe down the road, when I'm less energetic, more beset with health issues, and no longer able to go out drinking and dancing three nights a week, I'll reconsider becoming a Spring Hill volunteer in another or additional role. Until then, I vow to just say "no" and remain as uninvolved as possible. Unless. . . . I find that I miss the entertainment value of all the neighborhood spats, power struggles, and shenanigans.

CHAPTER 29

Who Will Be Next?

I was stunned when my neighbor Deidre passed away. I had liked Deidre. A lot. She was outgoing, effervescent, and the friendliest toward me out of all the neighbors I'd met. I'd found her difficult to talk with, however, since she was almost deaf. "What?" she'd yell at me, a big smile on her face. "I can't hear you." Still, I felt like she and I communicated, especially when she'd grab my arm and tell me what a good worker I was. Everyone likes recognition, even if it's only for how well they've cleaned off a table of dirty plates and coffee cups, right?

I only know a few of the neighbors in my little section of Spring Hill. There's Callie across the street, next door to the very unfriendly woman who won't speak but whom I saw carted away on a gurney as she texted on her phone. Initially, Callie hardly ever spoke to me, probably because she didn't see me. She usually walks with her head down, watching the sidewalk. I sort of feel like she's my friend. One time I gave her a container of homemade split pea soup for her and her husband, and she exuded enthusiastic thanks. However, she follows me religiously on Facebook, so perhaps that's enough. Trust me, I'm thankful for every hint of friendliness I can find around here. But I occasionally ponder over this rather unbalanced relationship, the one in which I know almost nothing about her, and she knows lots about me, thanks to my shameless and unrelenting posting on social media.

My favorite of all the neighbors, Winifred, lives next door to Callie. With the cold and rain of winter now upon Eugene, I don't see Winifred as often as I had in the warmer months. When I see her walk to the mailboxes with her walker, I'm always tempted to run out to talk with her for a few minutes, but I don't dare, lest I keep her outside in the cold too long.

A few weeks earlier, first responders had carted Deidre off to the hospital. Deidre had been home about a week when I caught Winifred on the sidewalk one afternoon. "How's Deidre doing?" I'd asked her.

"Oh, she's as sassy as ever," Winifred said. "She's had family staying with her a lot lately."

I'd seen all the extra cars in her driveway. My friend Polly had told me hospice was providing services, but Winifred did not volunteer this information.

"Did you go to the coffee last Saturday?" Winifred asked. When I said no, Winifred said, "You would have seen Deidre if you'd gone. As swollen as her feet and legs were, she managed to get herself across the street and help set up the pastries for the get-together." Winifred laughed. "There's just no keeping Deidre down."

Deidre had to have known she was dying. With the introduction of hospice, doctors stopped all but palliative care. I hadn't seen Deidre in several weeks, but neighbors told me her body had become bloated. She was no longer able to process toxins because of cirrhosis of the liver, and her heart could no longer properly circulate blood due to congestive heart disease. Still, on her deathbed, Deidre arose and volunteered in the community kitchen to be with her friends and neighbors.

Deidre passed away five days after that Saturday morning coffee. I'm sorry now I hadn't gone. I'll always remember how cheerful and happy she'd been at those get-togethers, socializing with her friends and making it a point to meet new attendees.

I was aware of at least a half dozen deaths in Spring Hill since Michael and I moved in. So far, Deidre had been the only one I'd personally known. Deidre had found something in this community I'd not yet discovered, obviously, based on her devotion to the monthly Saturday morning coffee hours.

New neighbors seemed to move in weekly, and they settled into the homes previously vacated by neighbors I'd never met. As I thought more about Deidre, I wondered if I was making a terrible mistake blowing off those monthly get-togethers. The time could arrive sooner rather than later when an hour-and-a-half in the Spring Hill clubhouse on a Saturday morning might be my biggest social event of the month. It'd be sad to go down to the clubhouse five years from now and not know a soul.

The aloofness of our neighbors in Spring Hill was baffling. Except for the woman living directly across the street from us, none of the other residents turned their backs to go inside when they saw us coming on the sidewalk. It was more like after saying hello, they'd be ready to get back to whatever they were doing before we happened along and interrupted them. Although I generally think of myself as a fair conversationalist, with these folks I found myself having trouble knowing what to say after saying hello.

Locals had warned me that Oregonians essentially want to be alone. This could explain at least a part of the avoidance I sensed with my neighbors. What I perceived as aloofness they could possible view as normal behavior. I look at my next-door neighbor, Mary Lou, for example, and while she's friendly enough to say hello and ask how we're doing, I've never heard her volunteer a single bit of information about herself.

Mary Lou has entrenched herself deeply in the community, however. She's served on the social committee, and she and her friend Mildred maintain the clubhouse library. I don't think she's ever missed a monthly morning coffee or Friday night dinner unless she was out of town, and she faithfully attends the weekly Knit & Stitch for two hours every Wednesday afternoon in the clubhouse. She also attends weekly Tai Chi and bimonthly Bible study meetings. Bunco meets monthly, and she's a regular participant. She interviews new residents and writes blurbs about them for the monthly neighborhood newsletters. And she probably does other things of which I'm unaware.

Yet Mary Lou keeps a very low, behind the scenes profile, and I really like that about her. When I think about the folks that rankle me in this neighborhood, it's the outspoken micromanagers, the ones who know everything and who act as if they're in charge of everything that irritate me.

Shortly after moving in, several neighborhood women encouraged me to attend that weekly Knit & Stitch group. They said I didn't have to know how to crochet, knit, or do needlepoint to attend, that I'd be welcome to just come, sit, and visit. My friend Pat related a conversation she'd had with a husband in Spring Hill who told her she absolutely must become a part of the women's stitchery group. "My wife wouldn't dream of missing it, and I always encourage her to go, even if she's not feeling well. It just makes me feel so good to know that she'll have support from that group after I die," this neighbor told Pat. This man's fervent description of the group touched Pat to the point that she attended one of the meetings. "They were very friendly and welcoming," she told me afterwards, "but I doubt I'll go back."

So far, I haven't mustered the courage to attend. I have trouble sitting through a two-hour movie. I don't do any needlework crafts, and I think I'd find sitting and doing nothing but talking and listening extremely difficult. Still, whenever I engage in my virtual rehearsal for widowhood, I always think of that Knit & Stitch group and wonder if, once again, I might be shooting myself in the foot.

The oldest resident of Spring Hill, Madeline, celebrated her ninety-eighth birthday a few weeks ago. She continues to live alone and make her way to the clubhouse for those monthly coffees. Unfortunately, Michael has avoided the clubhouse during afternoon football games in the clubhouse, so I don't have current information on whether Madeline continues to go there to watch the Ducks.

Being such a huge Winifred fan, I ask myself why I avoid getting to know Madeline. A possible explanation dawned on me a short while back that might also explain the aloofness I sense in my neighbors.

I believe it takes great courage to reach out and befriend someone you know could die soon. When I look around my neighborhood, where most of the residents are in their seventies, eighties, and nineties, I hesitate to try to develop close friendships. I tell myself it's because these "older" people don't engage in the same kinds of activities Michael and I do. And I believe I'm right on this score—they don't go for happy hours at wine bars, they don't go to Mac's Restaurant & Nightclub to listen to live music and dance, they don't go hiking at the Arboretum, and there are only two other people in the park who I ever see riding a bicycle with any hint of seriousness.

If I'm looking around this little community, sensing the mortality of my neighbors and feeling reluctant to invest myself emotionally in relationships that may be short-lived, my neighbors could well be having similar thoughts about me. Michael and I are relative newcomers, and while neighbors might view us as veritable fonts of energy and activity, we could well be harboring fatal illnesses that'll manifest themselves soon. Perhaps the unfriendliness of this over-55 park has nothing to do with Michael and me personally, but everything to do with our impending mortality, which we share with the residents of the other 101 houses.

Deidre's death took a toll on me in ways I'm still discovering. It's disconcerting to have a neighbor die, just as it's alarming to see emergency vehicles coming into the neighborhood several times a week. Every time I glance out my kitchen window, from which I have an unobstructed view of Winifred's house, I feel a jolt of anxiety, lest I see red emergency vehicles out front. Just as I feel when I see them drive down the street in front of my house and turn the corner. Every time, without fail, I ask myself, "Who will be next?"

And every time, I think to myself, "Next time it could be Michael. Or me."

CHAPTER 30
Cat Fights

As much as I'd vowed not to get further involved in community politics, Mildred's revelation at a garden club meeting ago haunted me. She had reported, with glee, her strategy to feed stray cats in her backyard so they would not attack and eat the beloved birds that visited her backyard feeders. I knew Angela was livid when she'd find cats in her backyard—she complained about the dead birds and feathers around her feeder, the stench of feline urine and feces when they used her backyard as a litterbox, and how much they upset her aging dog, who could hear, smell, and see the cats when they came around.

The worst of the report was Mildred's excitement as she told the garden club members about her other nocturnal visitors. "Harold and I have a motion-activated video camera set up to monitor what comes to our backyard at night to feed. It's really exciting to watch the video feed each morning to see who came calling."

I swear I saw mouths drop and eyes widen from several neighbors sitting around the large table, which was four rectangular tables pushed together with seating for about twenty people.

"Well, who comes?" Someone blurted out the question we all wondered about.

Mildred smiled and paused before beginning again. "In addition to our regular four feral cats, we get possums and raccoons. Those animals all go there and feed together, not paying each other any mind at all. It's so much fun to see."

And what about the friggin' rats you're probably also feeding? I wanted to ask but didn't. We'd had several neighbors tell us that Eugene teemed with rats and that we should keep an eye out for infestations in the crawl space under our house. And aren't you aware, I longed to ask Mildred, that wild animals carry diseases, and that unspayed and unneutered cats multiply almost as prolifically as rabbits? You might have four cats now, but in six or eight months, you could have a dozen or more.

I pushed the entire cat issue out of mind until one morning, around eleven a.m. when Michael heard a screeching noise in our front yard. I raced from the back of the house and arrived in time to see the end of a cat fight just as the two ferals disengaged and ran off in opposite directions.

"They're getting braver," I said to Michael. "I saw that Siamese-looking one drinking water out of the puddle in the street a few days ago, and now he's gotten bold enough to cross the street and come in our yard. I've never seen the brindled one before."

Michael continued reading his iPad, apparently paying me no attention at all.

"Does it concern you that we've got stray cats in our yard?" I asked him.

"No, why would it? I don't go out in the yard anyway."

"You surely complained about that Juniper bush along the front walk, the one under the kitchen window. Remember how it smelled so strongly of cat urine when the sun hit it in the mornings? If we get feral cats in the backyard, you're not going to want to even go out on the back porch to use the grill. The entire yard will smell like that Juniper plant." I'd paid Manny to remove the plant last Spring, primarily because Michael found the odor so offensive.

It crossed my mind again how totally oblivious Michael could be about anything that didn't affect him directly. When we'd talked about stray cats before, I'd reminded him of a neighbor in Tampa who fed feral cats and how they seemed to overtake the neighborhood. One time, a feral cat had hissed through the screen of our pool cage and transmitted a feline virus to my adorable little cat Lucy, who was strictly a pampered, beloved, indoor cat.

I'm as big a cat lover as anyone. I'd had house cats almost nonstop for years. In fact, when Michael first started talking about RVing in 2015, I made it clear I'd never go off in an RV while we still had cats. Our three cats were older, and we'd recently lost one at the age of sixteen and a second at the age of thirteen. Little Lucy had been the only one left, and it was after she passed away at age nineteen that I agreed to us buying an RV. Only the messiness of a litter box and the hope that Michael and I would continue traveling, albeit not in an RV, kept me from rushing down to the animal shelter and adopting two kittens the minute after we signed the closing documents for our house here in Spring Hill.

I wondered how many folks who weren't a part of the garden club feeding-of-feral-cats reveal were aware that Mildred was feeding them in her backyard. I learned a couple of weeks later that at least one person, maybe a dozen for all I know, met with Jill, our park manager, and expressed health and safety concerns about the feeding of feral animals.

Two days before the next garden club meeting, a voice message went out to the entire community from Jill. "I've been made aware that there are cats roaming in our community, and I'm not sure whether they are strays or whether they belong to residents. I just want to remind you that all pets must be on a leash when outside, which applies to cats as well as dogs. If you own a cat, please adhere to our park rules and do not allow your cat outside unless leashed. And finally, do not feed or do anything to attract stray cats to our neighborhood. They can carry diseases which pose health concerns for both people and other animals. Thank you."

In the interim between garden club meetings, the former leader had stepped down and convinced my friend Pat and me to co-chair the meetings. While not being eager to assume this little leadership role, I reluctantly agreed, primarily because I loved talking about plants and wanted to see the club continue to meet.

At the garden club meeting two days after Jill's voicemail, the meeting began as usual, and I didn't sense any hostility or dissention. We went around the table, as usual, giving everyone a chance to talk about what was happening with their plants. When Mildred's turn came, however, things took a different twist. Suddenly all hell broke loose.

"Well, I think we all heard Jill's voicemail on Tuesday, and, of course, we know exactly where Jill's information came from," Mildred said, her eyes fixed on Angela with undisguised vitriol.

"Why are you looking at me?" Angela retorted. "I haven't talked to Jill."

"Oh, come on, Angela," Jenny piped in. "We all know you're the one who complained."

"I swear to you, I have not talked to Jill," Angela almost screamed her denial.

"I really can't believe you're so intolerant of a little cat poop in your yard," Jenny said, a sneer on her face.

"I'll tell you right now," Mildred said, "that I will not abandon the feeding of those cats until the one that's injured has recovered. I went to Bi-Mart and bought a huge bag of the cheapest food I could find, and I'm going to start weaning them to take care of themselves. But the biggest cat, the Maine Coon, is walking on only three legs. He wouldn't be able to hunt and fend for himself right now."

"I don't think they're feral cats anyway," Jenny said. "I think they were domesticated and lived inside, probably in the apartments down the street. When the owners moved, they just left them behind. It's really tragic."

My memory fails on how the rest of the meeting unfolded. Eventually we moved on from Mildred's turn to speak to the next person sitting at the table. I felt unsettled and upset when the meeting ended and slipped out at once. Perhaps the strongest reaction was to suddenly realize that perhaps these cats weren't feral, teeming with parasites, and harbingers of disease after all. They were possibly gentle, tame, and beloved house cats whose owners had betrayed them.

A couple of days later, after my thoughts had jelled and my emotions had calmed, I said to Michael, "You know, I have an idea, and maybe I should talk with Mildred about it. What if the community pitched in together to solve this problem? We could get traps, capture the cats, everyone could chip in for veterinarian care to make sure they're healthy, and then we could try to get folks in the neighborhood to adopt them. There are only four, according to Mildred." I paused, knowing what Michael's reaction was going to be to my next sentence. "I'm going to claim the Maine Coon."

"No." Michael said. "We don't need cats again. They used to make it so hard to get away, even for a weekend. Not again."

Jeez, I thought. I can't seem to win no matter what I do. I'd come up with what I saw as an excellent solution, only to now realize that what might save me in the eyes of the neighborhood might have serious negative repercussions on my marriage.

CHAPTER 31
What's Important Anyway?

I looked around our over-1600 sq. ft. house and cringed. We'd been in the house only a year and a half, and already it bulged with stuff we didn't need. I could say with things we'd never wanted, but obviously either Michael or I wanted every item in this house or it wouldn't be there.

Minimalism had felt so right to me when we lived in our RV. I confess to having had thoughts of moral superiority, advanced enlightenment, and a higher level of self-actualization when we had surrounded ourselves with only items essential for our daily lives. Several years back, we had visited the replica of Henry David Thoreau's cabin in Concord, Massachusetts, and I was a little freaked out to realize his cabin was about half the size of our RV. But then, Thoreau lived alone while Michael and I shared the RV, so maybe I could still feel self-righteous that I lived in about the same number of square feet as Thoreau had. I also needed to keep in mind that Thoreau went to his mother's house for many of his meals and that he took his dirty clothes to her once a week for her to wash. In contrast, Michael and I did all our own meal preparation, housekeeping, and laundry.

Our house now borders on cluttered. We bought a chest of drawers for the master bedroom to have storage for socks and underwear, but shouldn't there be something decorative to sit on top of that chest? I found something ornamental to put on top of the chest in less than two weeks, something that would be of no use whatsoever other than to collect dust.

The house came with dozens of nails still in the walls. "Hey," Michael had said, "rather than take out the nails and leave holes in the walls, let's just find something to hang on every nail."

I rolled my eyes. "I was thinking we could get some spackling paste and dab a pinprick in every hole. Then we wouldn't have to buy stuff to hang."

"But we won't have to buy anything," my excited hubby said. "I've got all these posters from music festivals that I can frame. We'll have a museum of relics from some of the really cool places we've been."

Did my husband not understand that framing cost many times over what we'd paid for the posters? When we had first gotten together decades ago, we both had teenaged children from earlier marriages. We kept our finances separated and split all the household bills fifty-fifty. It made sense then. Michael didn't want to support my children, and I didn't want to support his. I loved the arrangement and refused to combine our finances even after the kids grew up and no longer depended on us financially. Sometimes we disagreed on what constituted "household bills," and for me, framing concert posters was not something I'd have spent my money on. Just as the gardening projects were my responsibility, since Michael didn't care what the yard looked like.

I joined in the home decorating mission somewhat, but by the time our few saved things from our Florida home finally reached Eugene via a moving van, Michael had filled every major wall in the house with his framed concert posters. I had a beautiful macrame hanging attached to a piece of driftwood that I'd made years earlier, but I now had no place to display it. I shrugged at the time and stuffed the tapestry in the foyer closet. It was out of sight but not out of mind. I have every intention of replacing one of those music posters with my original, artistic creation. Sorry, Michael.

As we added more things to the household, I found myself sometimes pounding in nails and picture hangers to make new holes in the walls to accommodate the vintage items I'd salvaged from thrift stores. Mirrors and clocks were among my favorite finds. The house was indeed becoming more cluttered by the week.

I'd never lived in the Pacific Northwest before, and folks had warned me about the long, cold, and wet winters, saying that the Willamette Valley could go for weeks without the sun ever peeking through the clouds. Michael and I felt wonderful when our first April finally arrived to realize we'd weathered our first winter in Eugene just fine. We hadn't become stir-crazy and restless, and we had no signs of Seasonal Affective Disorders. Still, I was awfully happy when the weather warmed up, the sun shone daily, and my plants started growing and blooming.

As we approached our second winter in Eugene, I thought back to the preceding winter and thought of what I'd missed the most during those long gray days. Plants. Not only could I not work outside in my garden, many of the plants in my yard had gone dormant and disappeared. In Florida, plants lived outside year-round with little to no cold damage. Also, because of a twelve-month growing season, I'd never indulged in houseplants when we lived in the south. They were more demanding than landscape plants, plus they attracted insects, such as roaches, ants, silverfish, and spiders. I believed strongly back then that plants belonged outside in the ground.

I now have a new take on houseplants. A fire had been lit. I would fill the unused breakfast nook area in our large kitchen with potted plants. The area had two large eastern windows where the morning sun shone in until at least noon. Above the largest kitchen window was a half-moon picture window deep enough for four or five plants in 6" pots to line the sill. Of course, I'd need a ladder to take the plants back and forth to the kitchen sink for watering, but I was willing to risk a ladder fall and subsequent broken neck to add plants in that perfect Eastern exposure.

There was a large empty area on the kitchen counter behind the sink. Several smaller plants would fit and thrive in that sunny spot. I could even grow a Phalaenopsis on that kitchen counter; it would be an ideal place for a low-light orchid.

Why hadn't I thought of this before? For our second winter in Eugene, I would have plants to look at, to touch, to tend, and to love during those long dreary days.

"Oh, Michael, come look at my new plant stand. It doesn't look too hard to put together." I'd just opened a huge box containing all the slats and screws for a gorgeous wooden plant stand from Home Depot and could hardly wait to put it together. Then I could begin the glorious quest for beautiful and perfect plants for the breakfast nook of my large, airy kitchen.

I couldn't believe how joyful that plant stand made me feel, or how exciting it was to find a common little Peperomia or Jade plant or any other of the hundreds of houseplants I'd grown through the seven-plus decades of my life. It was as if the 'real me' was re-emerging. Maybe the past few years have involved too many changes, too many losses, and too many horrors. Every time I added another small plant to the collection, I felt happier and more relaxed.

I suddenly saw an effective strategy for easing myself happily and easily through the final years of my life. I would focus only on things that brought me joy, as Marie Kondo had recommended in *The Life-Changing Magic of Tidying Up: The Japanese Art of Decluttering and Organizing*, her bestseller that I loved almost as much as Henry David Thoreau's *Walden*. Michael had never understood this, and I'm not sure others would either since it was not something I would ordinarily just insert into a conversation, but of all the pleasures and feelings of accomplishment in the entire universe, I'm not sure anything could top the joy of a plant that I'd nurtured from a seedling develop into an exquisite, near-perfect specimen.

I stood and stared for a long time at the neanthe bella palm that I'd bought over a year ago. It'd been my first Eugene houseplant, and at that time I'd decided to stop with just that one plant. I'd put the palm on the kitchen counter behind the sink. Within a year, it had doubled in size. I repotted it in the spring, and now it has almost doubled in size again and is in bloom. I'd never seen one bloom before, and to think it happened in my low humidity house in Oregon when the plant's native home was in

Southern Mexico and Guatemala left me in awe. The frigging thing was gorgeous. I vowed to keep repotting it until it reached my 8-ft. ceiling.

I loved plants, and maybe now that I lived in Oregon, I needed to focus on houseplants, for those I understood and could grow without the help of my buddy Manny, who was possibly going to take Carmen and their daughter on a very nice vacation this summer, thanks to all my special, financially lucrative projects that I tossed his way.

I was on to something. Growing houseplants was a far easier proposition than starting afresh in my mid-seventies to landscape a big yard. Whatever had I been thinking? I'd spent over a year of time and a veritable fortune building patios and planting hundreds of dollars' worth of landscape plants, trying to recreate the yard I'd had in Florida but with new-to-me plants that supposedly would thrive in the Willamette Valley.

Back in the early 1970s, I attended an Esalen Institute workshop on Long Island, NY. I remembered a truism from EST: Life is easier when you sit in the direction your horse is going.

At my age, I didn't have much time left in the saddle. Obviously. Probably not enough time to plant all these trees, shrubs, and perennials I'd been drooling over. But what if I concentrated on indoor plants, a gardening specialty with an almost 100-percent transfer of learning from Florida to Oregon?

With houseplants, I'd have almost total control over all facets of the collection—choice, temperature, light, watering, potting medium, feeding, and repotting. I could think of only two variables that wouldn't be the same. One would be the long, overcast winters with little to no sun for weeks at the time, though I supposed I could install grow lights. The second would be humidity. In Florida, with the air conditioning running twelve months of the year, the humidity would hover around 65% to 70%. Here in Oregon, even during the rainy winters, our humidity inside the house struggled to get above 40%. In the summer, it would sometimes drop as low as 20%, which would be okay for cacti and succulents but not for the lush, tropical foliage I wanted to grow. I realized humidifiers were not that expensive, and I could easily hide them behind large specimen plants.

I looked again at the now-over-two-feet-tall palm on my kitchen counter and smiled. I'd be more realistic going forward, setting goals and standards appropriate for someone my age.

That said, I wasn't looking forward to Michael's reactions as I filled the entire inside of our house with plants. I might not be able to physically move down to Costa Rica and live in a rain forest, but I could create an environment that felt somewhat similar right here in the Willamette Valley. At my age, I needed to concentrate on things that were important to me, and these days plants soothed my soul.

CHAPTER 32
My Summer as a Pimp

During the three years Michael and I lived in our RV, I missed the social connections I'd had when we lived at a fixed address. The pandemic contributed to my sense of isolation, but even with ongoing, outdoor, in-person group gatherings in campgrounds, the connections with others felt limited, shallow, and somewhat contrived. I longed for friendships in which we'd share intimate details about our lives. I wanted to know and be known.

Enter the Summer of 2023 in Eugene, Oregon, this mind-boggling period in which I came to know almost more about other people than was comfortable to know. The revelations and sharing of intimate details went only in one direction, however, and Michael and I were the recipients rather than the revealers. (I fully understand that anyone watching me or Michael might have viewed our choices with just as much interest as we viewed the activities of others.)

I innocently introduced a couple of single senior men to a few single senior women and then lived through weeks of detailed accounts from multiple directions of older people trying to forge romantic relationships. It might have been my social work listening and encouraging skills that kept these participants and observers running to me with every update, or it might have just been the result of having been the

179

one to set a couple of these romantic trysts into motion by introducing these folks to each other.

Michael dubbed me "The Pimp." I argued vehemently against the label. "I'm not trying to set up anything with anybody," I argued. Nevertheless, sordid, tawdry, and sometimes uncomfortable anecdotes seemed to enter my orbit via Messenger, text, and telephone several times a day. Did these people not have long-standing friends with whom they could gnaw all this stuff around with?

I was the new kid in town, and a somewhat happily married one who had zero interest in the dating world. All I wanted was to sit at my laptop, dig in my yard, read books, and enjoy a few board games with my hubby. And, of course, imbibe in red wine and Salty Dogs to my heart's content, or until I decided I'd better stop since I was the designated driver in our family. A ticket or an accident was the last thing I wanted.

By the end of the summer, I had experienced multiple epiphanies of the challenges of romance after age sixty-five. At times I found myself weary of the minutiae of unfolding events in the lives of these love seekers. Other times, however, I thought of myself as a scholar of the powerful drive that spurred my otherwise well-functioning friends towards doomed connections. While Michael will forever believe I spent my summer pimping for my friends, I choose to believe I supported my friends while engaged in natural field research.

🛺

"I'm calling to let you know I just got off the phone with the FBI," Jeremy said when I answered the phone. It'd been a couple of weeks since we had heard from him. He was in an RV park somewhere along the northern perimeter, making his way towards New Jersey to visit his stepson and his family. The phone jarred our morning routines of coffee (for Michael and me), writing (for me), and national news (for Michael).

"What?" I practically screeched my alarm into the phone. Although Jeremy was no longer in Eugene, we still kept in touch, and I certainly didn't want anything bad to happen to him. I assumed this FBI involvement had to do with his search for a companion. I was right.

I raced to the dining room, punched the speaker button on my phone, and motioned for Michael to pay attention.

"Yeah, it was sort of alarming for me, too." Jeremy chuckled. "I made the mistake of giving my cell phone number to this woman I connected with on Hinge, one of my online dating sites. She wanted to switch to this other app so we could talk on the phone rather than going through the Hinge chat room. It's not an uncommon way of communicating if you think you're clicking with someone, but I guess I made a mistake with this one."

"Why? What happened?" Michael asked.

"Everything seemed to be going well in the conversation for the first ten minutes or so, but then she abruptly switched topics and wanted to talk about cryptocurrency. When I told her I wasn't interested, she got really mad, like belligerent. So, I hung up, sort of kicking myself for not having seen that one coming."

"But you've encountered the crypto sellers before, right?" I asked.

"Yeah, several times. But I've never woke up the next morning and found a death threat on my phone. I'm in a campground in South Dakota, and I know rationally there's no way that woman could possibly find me. Still, it shook me up enough that I called local law enforcement. I also called the FBI, since I assumed the woman was across state lines."

"Wow. What did the cops say?" Michael asked.

"I first called the local sheriff's department and talked with a deputy, who said there was nothing his department could do and that the threat was nothing for me to worry about. He wouldn't even write up a report, so that's when I decided to call the FBI. This was yesterday, and an FBI agent called me this morning. While he assured me I'd done the right thing to report this, he agreed with the local folks that there's no way these crooks could ever find me and that I could relax."

Wanting details, I asked, "What did the message on your phone say?"

"It was a text that said 'Come outside and you die . . .' While common sense assured me there wasn't anyone outside waiting for me, I did look out all the windows and exited cautiously when I went out to my truck." Jeremy laughed. "It's certainly given me something to think about."

Not that I needed it, but Jeremy's message and phone call gave me more things to think about, too. Things I would have been happier not thinking about. I would have been terrified if anyone had left a death threat on my cellphone. I felt a great concern for my friend and hoped desperately this kind of drama would end soon. If it was rattling my bones, I could only imagine how stressful it must have felt for Jeremy.

Enter Brad, who now took my mind off Jeremy's adventures. Yes, Brad my idol, the man whom I thought was perfectly happy tootling around in his RV, all alone, with family and friends spread out from coast to coast. The one who'd shattered my perception of him by saying, in Jeremy's presence, that he'd like to meet 'some of these grandmas' who kept popping up on my Facebook posts.

Since Jeremy had left Eugene to RV his way to the other side of the country, Michael and I somehow started inviting Brad to go with us to hear live music when we went with our friends. The first invitation was to join us at Bennett Vineyards for a late afternoon blues concert, where we'd join our friends Chloe and Ruby. Chloe was my bicycling buddy, the one who'd watched me topple over in downtown Springfield for no apparent reason other than my klutziness, and Ruby was Chloe's next-door neighbor. Ruby wasn't really in the "running," as she was a full-time caregiver for her husband, who was dying of cancer. Chloe, in contrast, fit all of Brad's criteria, though in my mind she was so far out of Brad's league that he'd have been delusional to even think she'd look in his direction.

I stand corrected, however. Not only did Chloe look in Brad's direction, but she even opened the door for a Facebook connection. While Brad was clearly thrilled, he somehow managed to end the evening with Ruby's phone number but not Chloe's. I listened several days to Brad's texted lamentations of his missed opportunity and his pleas that I intervene on his behalf to throw in some kind and encouraging words to my friend Chloe on his behalf. "Sorry, Brad," I texted back. "I am not going there."

How fickle the fates. Enter my friend Maggie into Brad's world. The very same Maggie that our friend Jeremy had ignored in favor of Shelley, his karaoke queen. The same Maggie whom Jeremy believed had gotten into a beef with Shelley, being jealous that he was paying more attention to Shelley than he was to her. The very same Maggie whom I happened to know would never have wanted a man in her life more than a couple of days a week, at most.

I'm the one who introduced Brad and Maggie, never dreaming she'd give him a second glance. Maggie had invited us to Mac's to hear a blues band, and I asked if it was okay for Brad to come, too. "Of course," she'd said. "The more the merrier." While Maggie and Brad sat at opposite ends of a table of six that evening, somehow the charged ions traveled that distance, and by the next afternoon, Brad ecstatically reported that he and Maggie were going hiking together the following day.

Maggie and Brad's "involvement" lasted about a week. During that time, they both reported via text to me that they were having fun getting to know each other. They hiked, they met for dinner a couple of times, they volunteered together at a local food bank stuffing food into 300 children's backpacks, Brad helped Maggie attach new hardware on a vintage dresser she'd refinished, and they attended a park ranger's talk about Monarch butterflies. I felt somewhat awed as Brad chalked off their activities. Everything sounded so wholesome, so memorable, and so wonderful. Until it wasn't . . .

"She just dropped me," Brad said. "I'd texted on Tuesday to ask if we could get together Thursday afternoon. She didn't answer until Wednesday afternoon, and then it was to say, 'I'm busy all day on Thursday.' No explanation at all."

It'd take a few more days before Maggie gave me her explanation of what had happened.

🛺

Michael and I recently hosted our first Eugene house party with twenty-five of our new Eugene friends attending. Brad, Maggie, and Chloe were all on our guest list. As was Paul, one of Maggie's friends who was recently widowed. We had met Paul at the same blues concert where Brad had met Maggie. At our party, to my amazement, Maggie, Brad, and Paul all acted as if they'd never laid eyes on each other. I saw Chloe making the rounds and talking at length with both Brad and Maggie. She didn't talk with Paul; perhaps she didn't know him? But another amazing observation is that Maggie didn't talk with Paul either, and I knew they'd been good friends in the past.

What made the lack of communication between Paul and Maggie particularly noteworthy is that Michael and Paul had met for breakfast a couple of days earlier. Over bacon and eggs, Paul told Michael that he and Maggie were taking a trip together to a two-bedroom cabin in the mountains of Nevada to see the dark sky, information I filed away in my brain. As Maggie left the party that night, I walked out with her and mentioned her upcoming trip with Paul. "What???" she shrieked. "I told him no, that I would not go on that trip with him."

The next day, I texted Brad with my observation that he and Maggie had acted like they didn't know each other at the party. "Yes, I'm afraid I acted very childish," Brad said. He then called and gave Michael and me an almost hour by hour account of all the time he and Maggie had spent together, with who said and did what. He had no idea why Maggie had suddenly cut off all communication with him three days earlier; he only knew she had hurt his feelings and made him angry.

Maggie wanted to talk, and when we finally connected on the phone, she related her side of the story. "We were at my house, and he'd helped me with the hardware on a dresser. He asked if he could use my computer since he had no internet service at his RV park. I said sure, and I lay down on the sofa, thinking I'd nap for fifteen minutes." She paused. "Well, I ended up sleeping two hours, and when I woke up, he was just sitting there staring at me. It sort of creeped me out."

"WTF?" Michael later verbalized the reaction that'd been spinning in my mind for the past hour. "Who would go to sleep and leave a near-stranger sitting at her computer? He could have accessed financial records, retrieved passwords, and wreaked who-only-knows what other mischief if he were that kind of dude."

"But if he'd left while she was asleep, that would have really looked suspicious. She'd have spent the next month trying to figure out if he'd stolen something from her," I said. "I do know what you're saying, though. But if there'd be anyone I barely knew whom I might trust, it'd be Brad. Regardless of this dopey desire to couple up, I'd put my life on his honesty and integrity." I paused. "Still, I don't understand why he didn't just shake Maggie and wake her up. That's crazy to sit there two hours watching someone sleep. That'd creep me out, too."

Poor Brad, I thought. The way I saw it, Maggie had left him in an impossible situation. From Michael's perspective, Brad came across as needy. As I thought more about all that Maggie had told me, I remembered that she'd used the term 'clingy' at one point to describe Brad. But at the same time, just as with Shelley and Jeremy, I felt Maggie had encouraged Brad. Why else would they be hiking, stuffing children's backpacks, listening to park ranger presentations, and doing all these other things together? But then I realized that Maggie had lots of platonic friendships with guys. I could easily believe she'd been pursuing friendship as Brad dreamed of romance. I wasn't sure what my bottom line was in this confusion over motives.

Back to our party, Michael and I were both too busy during the seven-plus hours of entertaining to track all these fifty-, sixty-, and seventy-year-olds and their mating dances. I did overhear Chloe inviting Brad to a party at her house on Labor Day. The next day, Brad asked me if Maggie would be at Chloe's party. "Not to worry," I said. "You'll be safe. Maggie and Chloe don't hang out that often. Maggie will not be there." I could almost hear Brad's sigh of relief through cyberspace.

"What I don't understand," Michael later said to me, "is why your sympathies seem to be more with the desperate men than with these women who are your friends."

"And what I don't understand is how come you don't see how both Shelley and Maggie might have sent mixed messages to both Jeremy and Brad. They both came on very strong and then abruptly shut the guys off. You don't think they at least owed these men the courtesy of explanations?"

"I think both Jeremy and Brad were trying too hard. Ghosting was perhaps the best way of cutting it all off. It was certainly kinder than telling those guys what they might have been thinking."

"How can you be such a brute?" I asked. "Nothing happens in a vacuum. Absolutely nothing. Both Shelley and Maggie baited these men and then dropped them like they had leprosy. That's cavalier and callous, if you ask me, and it makes me mad."

My husband shrugged and returned his attention to whatever political commentary he'd been reading on his iPad. And I realized my interpretations could be just as misguided and off-the-wall as I considered Michael's to be.

Jeez, I thought. I'm not sure how I ever got myself involved in these soap operas, but I've got to extricate myself ASAP. These people are acting more adolescent than adolescents act, and they're taking up far too much of my time.

Meanwhile, Kathleen from our over-55 community caught Michael on the sidewalk to say she and her boyfriend Tim wanted to go to a vineyard with us sometime soon. I cringed to imagine how tales of our blues club, wine bar, and brewhouse pursuits of live music might be spreading among our neighbors. I was Facebook Friends with perhaps eight or ten of our Spring Hill neighbors, and I shamelessly posted photos on Facebook a couple of times each week from our various outings to hear live music. The photos usually included wine and beer glasses sitting in front of us on the table. I could only hope our neighbors didn't view us as raging, degenerated alcoholic psychos.

We set a date with Kathleen and Tim for the next afternoon when our favorite local musician would be playing at Sylvan Ridge Vineyard.

We didn't know Kathleen and Tim well, only that Tim was a disabled veteran and dying from cancer. Kathleen had let him move into her home a year-and-a-half earlier, and they'd talked about getting married. Per her own report, Kathleen had only known Tim a couple of months before they started living together. She added as an aside that Tim had never paid a penny of rent or bought a single loaf of bread to help with expenses. Now Tim's health was in a nosedive, and Kathleen found herself in the unpleasant and reluctant role of being an almost full-time caregiver.

When Kathleen had first told me this story, I could only say, "Wow." Later, I'd wondered aloud to Michael why anyone would have allowed a near-stranger with cancer to move into her home. It later occurred to me that Kathleen's response to Tim was totally opposite from Shelley and Maggie's behaviors toward Jeremy and Brad. Kathleen had found a needy man, taken him in, and assumed a caregiver's role. Shelley and Maggie had found needy men, teased them into thinking there might be a future between them, and then dropped them like hot potatoes.

I wondered what this interpretation of these situations said about me. Think I might be somewhat of a cad? Well, maybe.

🛒

Chloe's Labor Day party was fun, and the women outnumbered the men about two to one. However, Brad only had eyes for Chloe. He was the first to arrive at the party and the last to leave, except for three of Chloe's women friends, who had jumped into her hot tub. The next day, Brad called to ask whether I thought he'd made a mistake by not staying to help Chloe clean up.

It might have been that very moment when I realized I'd heard enough about the dating exploits of Jeremy, Brad, and Kathleen and Tim, although in the case of the latter it was the woman sharing the details rather than the men.

Sh*t. I could hang out a shingle and call myself a dating coach if I kept this up. I was up to my eyeballs with all these people's stories, and I wanted out. I could care less about who hung out with who or whether sparks ever flew between or among any of these people. Brad was the worst with the texts or calls three times a day, wanting to tell me what'd happened and asking me what I'd thought. I was ready to scream, "I don't think anything about what you're telling me," I silently screamed. "I've got my own life to live, and I'm totally sick of hearing about yours. Please just go away."

Neither Kathleen nor Tim showed up for the house party Michael and I threw. Seems that Kathleen had kicked Tim out of her house the day before and then taken off to visit family in Idaho. Based on the information I had, their situation made me feel heavy and sad. Tim was possibly a first-class loser and mooch, and even though he was dying from cancer, my sympathies were more with Kathleen than with Tim. However, I could only imagine the intensity of pain they both must be in. If there was blame and responsibility to assign, I suppose my bottom line would be to place it on Kathleen's shoulders for impulsively letting him move in and not dealing with his financial failure to chip in with expenses in the first week of their cohabitation. I wasn't sure how all these women could continue to invoke my criticism and these clueless men continue to garner my sympathies. My greatest relief, however, was that I'd not been the one to introduce Kathleen and Tim and that neither of them would be contacting me for advice or for my take on their situation. This time, thank goodness, I was not involved.

Less than a week later, Tim's truck was back in Kathleen's driveway. Although I initially sighed that my life of hearing romantic updates from my Spring Hill neighbor was obviously not quite over, I was wrong. That episode was over, and we never heard another word from Kathleen. About a month later, we heard that Tim had passed away. Seems that Kathleen had sent him back to his own house in Coburg to die.

Somehow, I felt relieved that I'd not been privy to the excruciating details of Tim's final days. Six months later, Kathleen had another man's SUV permanently parked in her driveway.

I remembered my hubby's wise words: The assholes are equally distributed between the sexes.

CHAPTER 33
Old Lady Options

A few weeks ago, I made a $50 donation to the Arbor Day Foundation. I'd joined enough plant societies, garden clubs, and online plant groups since settling down in Eugene and I'd attended enough in-person gardening events and programs for my name to somehow make its way to the Foundation's mailing list.

I succumbed to the organization's excellent marketing strategy for coaxing donations out of tightwads like me. For a mere $25 donation, they would send me ten free trees, two free crepe myrtles, and one tree planting guide. What a haul for twenty-five bucks. I wanted to believe my love of trees prompted me to throw in an extra $25 to my donation, but that was only part of the explanation.

After all the money I'd spent during the past year on landscape plants for my new yard, I was ready for a bargain, and this seemed like the bargain of the century. The promised windfall of bounty motivated me more than my love of trees until I read the fine print, at which point I wondered if I'd been truly scammed. The ten free trees were a mere six to twelve inches in height and most likely bareroot, although the flyer didn't specify that. The tree collection included two Flowering Crabapples, three Eastern Redbuds, two Washington Hawthorns, and three White Flowering Dogwoods. I'd always thought of crepe myrtles as small trees, but I guess the Arbor Foundation considered them shrubs. The Foundation said all these plants were Oregon natives and selected especially to thrive in my hometown. Wow.

Several weeks later, I wondered what I was thinking with my $50 donation and promise of all those trees and shrubs. I looked at my small yard, currently bereft of a single tree since the previous owner had hated trees and had cut them all down. I had room to plant maybe two or three small trees at most. Oh, well . . . maybe my neighbors will start speaking to me if I start giving away trees, even if they are only teeny-weeny bareroot seedlings.

It dawned on me soon after my check went in the mail that I'd failed to consider a very important factor. The important issue was not my limited space but rather the limited number of years I had left to live. If I'd obsessed over whether I was too old to plant blueberry bushes, and I had indeed obsessed ad infinitum, I was truly nuts to even think about planting trees. At the speed with which trees grew, maybe that little crabapple would reach my knee before I kicked the bucket. I'd certainly not live long enough to enjoy an apple cobbler for my efforts.

Later I learned that folks plant crabapple trees for the birds and the environment, not for edible apples for human consumption. That knowledge only slightly dampened my spirits, and I refused to abandon hope that someday I'd pick apples in my backyard and bake a delicious cobbler.

A couple of days after the realization that I was possibly too old to plant trees registered in my shriveling, deteriorating brain, I had an appointment with my endodontist for a cleaning. Although I'm blessed with relatively good teeth, I nevertheless dread the quarterly cleanings that both my dentist and my endodontist believe I need.

Shortly after I settled in the chair and the hygienist started working, I found myself wondering why I was going through this at my age. What if I just stopped going to dentists altogether? How many years could I go before I get into trouble? Could my good dental health last me the rest of my life if I never went back to see a dentist again after today?

My mind drifted as the hygienist continued poking, scraping, and polishing in my mouth. I really enjoy pinot noir, I thought, so why at seventy-five should I even be counting the number of days each week I indulged or how many glasses I drank each day? And when I wasn't drinking red wine, I thoroughly enjoyed Salty Dogs. I thought of both drinks as brilliant and efficient ways to squeeze into my diet extra servings from the fruit and vegetable food group. After all, those expertly fermented grapes from Oregon and that wonderful freshly-squeezed grapefruit juice from Florida were both fruits and undoubtedly loaded with vitamins and minerals that were good for my health.

I don't often enjoy cooking, so why am I reluctant to eat out in restaurants? Michael and I could afford to eat out, so it wasn't about the money. It was about the sodium, the fat, and all the additives and chemicals. Sitting in that dentist's chair, I realized I needed to consider the same question that I'd asked about planting blueberries and crabapple trees. Why should I worry at my age about putting unnatural chemicals in my body? I probably wasn't going to live long enough for it to even matter.

This is fun, I realized. I should start making lists of all the things I do that I'd rather not do, and then I should muster the courage to stop doing them. Or alternatively, what are the things I'd love to do that I've avoided since they wouldn't be good for my health? Maybe when I leave this dental appointment, I'll swing by Voodoo Doughnuts and buy a dozen warm glazed ones to scarf down on my way home.

I saw my podiatrist the day following my dental appointment. My poor feet were collapsing with severe osteoarthritis, and doctors as far back as fifteen years ago had recommended fusing the bones as the best solution. The big toes on both feet turned upward like an elf's toes, and my other toes had gnarled and curled in strange positions as they rubbed against each other when I walked. In the past, I'd been a 'wiker,' a term Michael had coined as being about halfway between walking and hiking. Five years ago, I could easily wike three or four miles a day. Now I'd reached the point that anything more than about two-and-a-half miles left shooting pains in my feet for hours after the walk ended.

Bad feet had led me to switch to bicycling as my preferred way to get my pulse rate up a bit. Now, six months later, my feet seemed to have deteriorated even more, thus leading to this podiatry appointment.

"I think the bicycling is probably hurting your feet," my new podiatrist said. "You'd be much better off on a stationary bike in a gym."

"What?" My blurted response came involuntarily. "But I love riding my bike, and I love being outside in the fresh air and the sunshine. I don't want to exercise in a gym. How could bicycling be making my feet worse?"

"It's the stopping and starting that's stressful," the doctor said, talking to me in the patient tone one might use with a child. "Every time you put your foot down when you stop, it's a jolt, and every time you push off with the other foot to take off, it's stressful for that foot. With your feet, bicycling is probably not your best form of exercise."

"I'm not happy to hear this." She'd just thrown me a major curve ball.

"Of course not. You want to do what you want to do."

And don't we all, I thought.

As I approached my seventy-sixth birthday, I realized that I'd probably keep on riding my bicycle no matter what this foot doctor told me. There are just a few things, like bicycling and gardening, that I would not give up, no matter what. And when I thought seriously about this subject, I realized that drinking alcohol might well fall into this same category of things to keep doing.

However, I must draw the line with some of the decisions I make as I get older. With pets, for example, and specifically with cats. I love the thought that Spring Hill could solve its stray/feral cat issue with a capture and adopt strategy, and I'd love to again adopt a rescue cat. I've been a cat owner and lover all my life, and a cat would bring me lots of joy and comfort as I continue my tromp into the sunset.

But at my age, adopting a kitten felt irresponsible. I would not want to commit to a pet that would likely outlast me. But wouldn't I be taking the same risk with a three- or four-year-old cat? How much time do I have left, and would it be conscionable at my age to consider a pet of any age? I do not think it would. It simply would not be fair to an animal to risk not being there for the duration of its life.

That said, Michael and I met a wonderful couple in an RV park one time who routinely adopted older Corgis and provided a loving home with good veterinarian care for their final years. I looked at this couple in amazement, and I've thought about them often. I'd been devastated when I'd lost my last three cats, not one of which did me the courtesy of passing away peacefully while sleeping at home. I'd had to have each one put down by the vet. I'd sworn with the last one that I'd never put myself in a position like that again. It was just too painful to lose animals I'd loved so much. I couldn't imagine all the old dogs that Corgi rescue couple had cared for, loved, and then bid farewell. I didn't think I could do it emotionally. And to be honest, I'm not sure I believed all those elderly Corgis appreciated living to the point they could hardly walk outside to do their business anymore. Surely there was room in the universe for a bit of mercy.

Though unplanned and unbeknownst to us until long after we signed on the dotted lines to become homeowners in Eugene, Michael and I had landed in a great state in which to grow old. Oregon is one of only ten states in the United States that allows physician-assisted death. The criteria are straightforward under Oregon's Death with Dignity laws. Patients must be over eighteen, diagnosed with a fatal condition with less than six months to live, and capable of choosing to die of their own free will.

I'm comforted to know I might have the benefit of an early release from pain, suffering, and exorbitant end-of-life medical expenses. I especially like the thought of being in control until the very end.

Maybe if I'm serious about making lifestyle adjustments and no longer plan to focus on doing everything possible to extend my life, I should think a bit more seriously about which pleasures to give up and which ones to continue embracing.

So far, I'm going to pass on adopting a cat, even an older one. I will continue to imbibe alcohol and ride my bicycle, though not at the same time. Both activities are fun and make me very happy.

I'd show no restraint at all if I swung by Voodoo Doughnuts and picked up a dozen, so I'll pass on that idea. I'll probably continue to show semi-good judgment with food choices, not because of the chemical additives as much as my desire to avoid adding more excess pounds than the ones I already carry. Thankfully, I have three more months before I must decide about those quarterly teeth cleanings.

Which leaves primarily only the decisions about plants, and because I'm a gardener, and because plants just might be my favorite thing in the world, I plan to continue planting things, even twelve-inch bareroot Flowering Crabapple trees because I believe in the future. If I can be as lucky as now-ninety-six-year-old Winifred across the street, I just might one day enjoy sitting in the shade of my own apple tree even if I'll never get an apple cobbler from it. Which reminds me, I'll have to ask Winifred what she did with that ONE big lemon on her little flower-laden lemon tree. While I'm at it, I might also ask her how often she has her teeth cleaned. I'd seriously like to drop dental care from my end-of-life regime.

My National Arbor Foundation bounty of ten trees and two crepe myrtles did not have an especially good ending. I didn't want the crepe myrtles and gave them both to neighbors. Neither one survived its planting. Of the ten free trees, I easily found homes for the three Flowering Dogwood trees, not one of which ended up living.

I ended up keeping and planting two Eastern Redbuds and giving the third one to my gardener Manny, who possibly tossed it out of his truck window on his way home. One of the Eastern Redbuds didn't make it, but the other did and grew to about 15" with a dozen or so leaves. When I expanded the patio area in my backyard, I had to pull up this surviving tree out of the ground for patio stone installation. Those little 12" Washington Hawthorn seedlings would reportedly grow into huge trees, and I could not find a single soul who would accept one. I ended up tossing them into my yard waste bin for recycling. My small yard barely had enough room for a little crabapple tree.

One of the two crabapple trees died, but the other one seems to be thriving. I was dead wrong to have questioned planting it. A year later, my little 12" twig is now over 2-ft. tall and has several branches and many leaves. Maybe I wasn't too old to plant this tree after all, though I won't hold my breath for the apple cobbler.

Postscript: In 2025, as Arbor Day approached, I received another letter from the Arbor Day Foundation. I looked at the return address, felt the heft of the envelope and knew it held another generous offer of trees, shrubs, a planting guide, and return-address stickers that I could proudly attach to my outgoing mail for a mere $25 donation. Should I feel apologetic that I tossed that envelope into the garbage without even opening it?

CHAPTER 34
Body Betrayals Abound

Although I wanted to see myself as indefatigable and immortal, I saw ir-
refutable evidence to the contrary. I was not as spry, active, and youthful
these days as I wanted to believe I was and certainly not as much as I used
to be. Sometimes I felt justified in yielding to a bit of self-pity. Getting
old was simply not fair.

The rational part of me knew my view of myself as young and vibrant
was a boldface lie. I'm falling apart physically, and my body is betraying
me in more ways than I want to count.

My hair was getting shaggy, and I needed a haircut. To keep it from
falling in my eyes, I sometimes took a couple of clips and pinned it back.
I used to wear my hair this way years ago and liked the way it accentuated
my high cheekbones, which my mother used to say reflected my Native
American DNA. Not that I believed I had a single strand of genetic in-
digenous coding anywhere in my body despite my maternal grandfather's
name of Wyoming Tecumseh Anderson. My maternal grandmother, who
claimed descension from a Hungarian princess, used to argue that Wyoming's mother had simply read a lot of cowboy and Indian stories, thus
explaining his ethnic-sounding name.

After securing my hair with clips, I grabbed my hand mirror and
examined my face in the mirror from all angles. I discovered, in horror,

that from a profile view, I looked as if I had no lips. They'd become so thin and drawn they were now invisible. My mother had very thin lips, and when she was upset or angry, her lips rolled inward and disappeared. Tight-lipped, I'd always thought. Unable to believe this profile of such a decayed and lipless old woman, I slammed the mirror back into the drawer. Already, the clips in my hair were beginning to slide out anyway. My hair had thinned too much to hold them secure, so I jerked the clips from my hair. I'd risk falling down stairs and walking into walls because of hair obstructing my vision before I'd present a startling image in public of a lipless old woman.

My lips weren't the only things that had disappeared from my body. Michael and I were avid Queen fans before Freddy Mercury passed away. Next to "Bohemian Rhapsody," "Fat Bottomed Girls" was one of our favorite Queen songs. Michael used to call me a fat-bottomed girl, but he wasn't serious. While I've always been a bit beefy in the arms and thighs, my butt had never been oversized. About a decade ago, I remember looking in the mirror and realizing my butt had disappeared. Flat as a pancake, which made jeans always feel a bit saggy in the rear and created the need to wear a belt.

I've discovered other physical losses, too. When I was younger, I had beautiful eyes with long curly lashes. Now I have small, squinty eyes, which bear an uncanny resemblance to my dad's. When I look in the mirror, I no longer see any eyelashes at all. I'd never waste money these days on mascara because I'd never be able to find enough lashes to apply it to. Which reminds me of the thick, bushy eyebrows I used to painstakingly pluck with tweezers and shape on my brow. They, too, have disappeared, with not a single hair left on my forehead.

Speaking of hair, of which mine has not turned particularly gray and thus has not led to any interest or perceived need to color, I remember well the times when hairdressers would exclaim over how thick my hair was despite its fineness. "You have an incredible number of stands of hair per square inch," they'd told me throughout the years. I struggle now to remember the last time anyone told me I had a lot of hair. Multiple strands come out every time I brush it. And it takes a very special barrette not to slide right out.

I've been luckier than many when it comes to dental health. So far, I've only had two root canals, three crowns, and one extraction, which dentists tell me is excellent for someone my age. But it's not all good news, unfortunately. Following the extraction, I'd had a bone marrow graft in preparation for an implant three months later. An endodontist in Florida did the graft, using marrow extracted from deceased felons within the Florida State Penitentiary System. (I sometimes wondered whether those criminal bone marrow cells had affected my world view or compromised my moral code in any way. I'm happy to report that I continue to have a squeaky-clean history with law enforcement.)

However, by the time the pandemic had ended and I was ready to proceed with the implant, my new endodontist in Eugene said, "Before we can proceed, we'll have to do a bone marrow graft because you've lost a lot of bone in your gums."

"But I've already had a bone graft," I said, shocked that he'd say such a thing. "Last year my dentist told me it looked good and that I was ready for an implant."

"Sorry, but it's gone away. There's not enough bone now to securely attach a post. It'll have to be done over."

"If it went away one time, what's going to keep it from disappearing again?"

The endodontist shrugged. "I don't know."

"Six thousand dollars is a lot of money to pay for a tooth way back in the top of my mouth that only you and I know is missing. I'm going to have to think about this a bit more."

Two years later, I'm still thinking about that gap in my mouth where a tooth used to be. I can crunch carrots, apples, and anything else I want on that side of my mouth with no difficulty, and I could probably spend a couple of fun weeks in Amsterdam for the cost of that implant. So far, I haven't called the endodontist to reschedule.

I won't go into full tilt reveal on all the other body parts that are deteriorating. My nails are brittle and cracked despite 5000mcg of Biotin daily. My skin is dry and flaky despite a daily slathering of Keri Bath Oil and Gold Bond Diabetic's Dry Skin Relief Body Lotion. I have black and purple splotches on my arms that make me look like a battered woman. My dermatologist tells me the splotches are simply skin damage resulting from bruises on top of bruises on top of bruises. He laughingly added that the common name for this condition is "rusting." Rusting! I almost screamed in disgust when he told me this. Of all the other things going on in my body, the idea of rusting was just about the end of my ability to process. (I'd totally freak out if my dad hadn't had the same kind of splotches, so again, it's another one of those familial aging signs that unfortunately feels familiar and inevitable. I'm thinking as long as my platelet count doesn't drop to 14, as it did for my dad, or as long as I don't develop ulcers on my legs that stay open and ooze for months on end like my older brother had, I should feel thankful.)

I won't dwell on the four squamous cell carcinomas dermatologists have diagnosed during the past five years, two of which had advanced enough to require Mohs surgery. Maybe it made sense that my skin, the largest organ in the body, should be the one failing me the most. I try to comfort myself by saying at least it's not my liver, thus justifying continued alcohol consumption to soothe the devastation triggered by unsightly skin covered with scars and discolorations. On a positive note about skin cancer, my last visit with my dermatologist was the first one in almost three years that didn't end up with multiple blisters from being zapped with liquid nitrogen, a bloody bandage from a biopsy of a suspicious area, or dire warnings to use sunscreen and return in six months or earlier for a recheck. I think this Oregon weather, with its long, overcast winters, has been a welcome reprieve from my earlier sun-filled years in Florida and in the deserts of the southwest.

My hearing is worse than ever despite hearing aids that supposedly bring it up to normal parameters. An audiologist explained to me decades ago that too many sounds, especially consonants, had been removed from my auditory library shelves.

My vision is also deteriorating. I now need to increase print size on my laptop to 120 percent to read comfortably. I silently call my ophthalmologist an idiot when he tells me my vision is 20/20 when wearing my glasses.

I feel helpless in the kitchen when it comes to opening jars and removing lids despite the multiple gadgets from Amazon jamming our kitchen drawers, all designed to make bottle-opening a piece of cake. I avoid jicamas, winter squashes, and fresh coconuts because I lack the strength in my hands to peel and process them.

Despite ergonomically designed gardening tools, I still struggle in my beloved yard with pruning and trimming small, tree-sized shrubs, like rhododendrons. My hands are weak and have trouble with pruners and lobbers. My skin is so thin that the slightest poke from a branch or limb breaks the skin and makes me bleed like someone stabbed me. It's hard to lift bags of mulch, especially when they're wet and weigh four times more than they should. Damn you, Lowes, with your half-priced mulch sale during which I stocked up with forty-five bags, hoping they'd last a year. The first batch of fifteen bags was fine when I got home and unloaded them to the garage. Why the hell were the last thirty bags sopping wet?

Before we left Florida in the RV, I donated blood regularly to the Red Cross. No big deal; it was just something I liked to do, and it made me feel good. Sometimes I'd even donated platelets in memory and in honor of my dad. In searching for ways to feel more a part of my new community here in Eugene, I optimistically went to the Red Cross website, filled out a questionnaire, and scheduled an appointment to donate blood. I felt so excited and smug—the blood mobile would be almost around the corner from my house, less than half a mile away.

I arrived early for my draw appointment, pleased to see I'd not have to wait. The first step, the one prior to the many questions relating to sexual behaviors, international travel, and health and medications, was the finger prick to see if my red blood count was high enough. Normal ranges are 12.0 to 15.00. On the first attempt, the nurse eked out a disappointing 11.9 from my pale red specimen. "I think we can do better," she said. "Our requirement is a 12.5." On the next attempt, she squeezed and squeezed my finger, and I assumed she was trying to get a 'deeper' reading by collecting blood that hadn't been circulating so close to the surface. Her additional efforts brought the reading up to a whopping 12.3. "Maybe eat a lot of iron-rich foods for a week or so before coming in again," she told me as I left, my head hanging in shame.

Back home, I emailed my primary care physician, expressing concern and asking if she thought I might be anemic. She ordered blood work, which came back with a 12.5 reading for my red blood count. "You're fine," she told me. "Stop worrying."

Still, the incident upset and depressed me, so much that I knew I'd never try to donate blood again. At my age, I figured I needed to keep every ounce of everything I still had inside my body. Things were deteriorating and disappearing fast enough without me voluntarily giving a single molecule of anything away.

I don't think anyone would ever think I had an abundance of testosterone. I'm softly spoken, easily intimidated, and don't always defend myself in situations where I feel overwhelmed and/or overpowered. I'm the one who quietly defies rather than openly confronts. Despite understanding intellectually that menopause triggers multiple hormonal changes, including a rise in the production of testosterone in female bodies, I was nevertheless unprepared and shocked when I began to see changes in my own body suggesting a rise in testosterone. I didn't mind so much that my hair changed from straight to curly, but the whiskers that began popping up sporadically on my chin totally freaked me out. Consultation with other women my age confirmed that this was common and would probably continue. In an overabundance of caution, I now have four tweezers stashed in handy locations so I can pluck any newly-discovered hair from my chin the minute I see or feel it. Better safe than sorry, eh?

The majority of my complaints and anxieties come from vanity and resistance to the inevitability of aging. I should not be throwing adult temper tantrums since I am healthier than I deserve to be, given my lack of self-control with calories, additives, and alcoholic beverages, and my somewhat inconsistent commitment to exercise.

Why can't I get a grip? All these piddly little things happening to my body are not big deals. If they are precursors to something horrific coming down the road, I probably should just feel relieved and happy that I don't yet have the big picture. While I hate pithy little sayings, when it comes to changes as one grows older, I believe that ignorance really might be bliss.

It might not be so bad to spend the rest of my life in La La Land.

CHAPTER 35

The Cane Dancer

"Why do we continue to obsess about all these old men trying to find love?" I asked Michael. We were getting ready to go to a Halloween costume party at our favorite Eugene venue for live blues. "I'm not sure I even want to meet Paul's new girlfriend."

"I'm not sure it's just the old men we're following here. Seems to me the women are about on par with the men in terms of numbers. For the men, we've got Jeremy, Brad, and Paul. And for the women, we've got Shelley, Maggie, and Kathleen. Sounds about even to me."

"Yeah," I said, "but the women check out a guy and then move right on along if it doesn't feel right. The men, in contrast, seem to perseverate."

"If I'm remembering correctly, it took Kathleen about two years to kick Tim out of her house. That's not exactly moving right on along, if you ask me," Michael said.

"I can't shake all those Paul stories, how he was on the prowl two months after burying his wife. All that crap he told you about him and Maggie planning to share this cabin under a dark sky in Montana and then Maggie going ballistic when I told her he'd told you that."

"Oh, there's another Maggie and Paul story I haven't told you about," Michael said. My husband and Paul met every few weeks for breakfast. I was pleased that Michael had found a guy friend to get together with. I'd not had much trouble connecting with women my age in this town and was happy that Michael had finally made a friend.

"Let's hear it, I guess. Although if we're going tonight so Paul can introduce us to his girlfriend, who you tell me he's madly in love with, then why are there still Maggie and Paul stories?"

"I couldn't begin to answer that," Michael said, exasperation in his voice. "Do you want to hear this story or not?"

"Okay, then. Let's hear the latest installment."

"A couple of weeks ago, Paul and Maggie both happened to be out at the same place in Santa Clara listening to music. Maggie was with a girlfriend, and Paul was by himself. Guess they didn't sell mixed drinks at this place because Maggie was drinking a beer. So, Paul comes over and tells Maggie he'd like to buy her a beer, and Maggie told him no thanks. Well, he ordered one for her anyway and walked over to deliver it to her. According to Paul, Maggie got furious and stormed out to her car to leave. Now comes the funny part," Michael said, pausing to catch his breath. "Paul goes running out after her and starts pounding on the car window as Maggie is backing out of the parking lot and screaming at him to go away."

This incident had occurred just few days before Michael and Paul met for breakfast, and according to Michael, that incident with Maggie was all Paul could talk about. Paul had been so upset that Maggie was mad at him, he went home that night and tapped out an almost 500-word text, to which Maggie never responded.

"Paul handed me his phone, wanted me to read what he'd written and see what I thought. It just went on and on, with Paul begging Maggie to please be his friend, that he'd not meant to offend her, and that he'd do anything if she'd just please accept his apology. It was really bizarre."

"We surely get the minutiae, don't we?" I remembered Brad and how he'd kept Michael and me on the phone, sometimes for an hour or more, reporting every single detail of conversations and things that'd happened the short week or so when he and Maggie had hung out. "Maggie certainly has no trouble attracting men, does she? Too bad she doesn't even want one, huh?"

"What do you mean?" Michael asked.

"I mean that my friend Maggie likes men just fine." I laughed. "To quote her, she'd love to have a man in her house, for maybe two or three hours a couple of nights each week."

"What's that supposed to mean?"

"I've been trying to tell you, Michael. None of my single women friends are looking for anything other than a good time. They spent years taking care of husbands and children, and now they don't want to take care of anyone but themselves. And all these guys are looking for serious relationships. There's a definite disconnect here, don't you think?"

The blues club held its Halloween Costume Party in the upstairs ballroom, and the music came from a half-dozen or so harmonica players having a blowout with assorted local musicians. Michael and I had dressed as a beekeeper and a queen bee, a rather "cute" pair of costumes that felt out of place amidst the adult costumes. Maggie, for example, came dressed as a naughty Catholic school girl and her friend Carolyn came as a mermaid in a skin-tight top that plunged all the way to her belly button. We saw dapper couples in Roaring Twenties flapper outfits, tuxedos and ballroom gowns, hippies in various states of free-love nudity, and other well-crafted and assembled costumes.

I'm not sure what Paul had intended to convey with his top hat, ill-fitting sport coat, and pants held up with suspenders. Paul's new love-of-his-life girlfriend had cobbled together an original costume with all sorts of recyclable items tied, pinned, or attached to her clothing. Her name badge said that she was the Queen of Recycling.

These clever and originally conceived costumes initially left me embarrassed at the Amazon ready-made costumes Michael and I wore. I quickly recovered, however, when I realized I'd been reading, writing, bicycling, and gardening, all activities that meant a hell of a lot more to me than a friggin' Halloween costume. I resolved to practice a bit more kindness toward myself. No one can do it all, and if I was doing things that were important to me, then I was on the right course.

Somehow my queen bee Halloween costume failed to inspire me to dance much at Mac's that night. Not sure whether it was Paul's costume, or excitement over having his new girlfriend (and showing her off to Maggie), or some other motivating factor that led Paul to dominate the dance floor, mostly by himself, although his girlfriend did get up and dance with him a few times.

Paul's energy surprised me, for he told us he'd been sick with covid a week earlier. Although he swore to us that he'd tested negative and his doctor told him it was okay if he went out, it surely made me nervous being in such proximity to him. He kept a mask on all night, but most of the time the mask hung under his chin, which did nothing to reassure me of my safety. Michael later learned that Paul's girlfriend had gotten so angry at him that night because he wouldn't keep his mask on that she almost broke up with him.

To understand Paul's dancing, an image of his physique is necessary. He's a rather physically small dude, maybe seventy-three or seventy-four years old. I'm not sure whether it's osteoporosis, scoliosis, pain from a severely arthritic hip that needed a replacement, or another physical impairment, but Paul walked stooped over at about a seventy-five-degree angle. He always walked slowly and with caution, and he used a cane for balance and support.

Paul's enthusiasm and intensity on the dance floor at Mac's that night astounded me, and I ended up wondering what he might have imbibed to supplement the two or three beers I'd seen him drink. When Paul started to dance, it was as if a younger, healthier, more robust spirit entered his body.

Paul's dancing triggered memories of my childhood days in the Deep South, a place where parishioners in Pentecostal churches became so overcome with the Holy Spirit, they yelled out their amens, swooned and occasionally fell to the floor, and spoke in tongues. On that dance floor on Halloween night, Paul's posture straightened up, and instead of using his cane for balance and safety, he swung it high over his head, whirled it around in the air, and pumped it up and down in time with the music. He danced as if an alien had transported him to another universe and some invisible force had such control over him it made me wonder if the Rapture had finally arrived.

Although Paul had supposedly told his girlfriend all about us and that she was looking forward to meeting us, Paul hardly acknowledged our presence in the ballroom that night, which again led me to question what intoxicants he might have been enjoying in addition to alcohol. Michael and I sat with our friends Maggie, Carolyn, and Cassidy at a table not far from where Paul and his girlfriend sat. Towards the end of the evening, Paul's girlfriend got up, walked over to us, and introduced herself. It proved so anticlimactic that I don't even remember her name, and I doubt that she remembers mine.

Driving home that night, I said to Michael, "There's something different about your buddy Paul. He's so self-absorbed that the external world doesn't even exist for him. Do you think he even noticed that he was out on that dance floor for hours, and that his girlfriend wasn't there with him?" I thought about it for a couple more minutes. "This whole thing about Maggie, maybe the dude just feels awful when he thinks he's hurt someone's feelings or somehow made a mistake about something, but he just doesn't fit the mold of Brad and Jeremy. I don't think Paul needs or wants anyone. It's like he's totally self-contained, oblivious to the world when he's out there dancing. Can you imagine experiencing that kind of abandon, being so in the moment you don't even notice whether you have a partner there with you or not?"

Michael didn't answer, and I assumed he either didn't know what I was talking about or he'd not paid any attention to me. That was okay. I needed some more time to process this, but somehow, I think this crazy coot Paul had stumbled upon some internal strengths that Brad and Jeremy either did not have or had not yet discovered. While my women friends, Maggie, Shelley, and Kathleen, didn't seem to be as desperate as the guys, they did not appear to have found that abandon that Paul had shown when he was on the dance floor that night at the Halloween concert, pumping his cane as hard as he could toward the ceiling, and for all outward signs, totally oblivious that there was even a world out there. His dancing felt like a perfect example of being happy with yourself, inside and out.

I wanted to know Paul's secret, for I knew the odds were great that someday I, too, would be an elderly person alone in the world. Maybe it didn't matter that Paul sometimes imagined promises from his friend Maggie that she had never made. That night of the Halloween party, he'd truly appeared to be one of the happiest free spirits I'd ever seen.

I would realize a few months later that Paul spent most of his waking time stoned to the gills. Bottom line, I realized, is that Paul was getting a little help from his friends.

Michael and I are still waiting for Paul to introduce us properly to his girlfriend. Paul sends Michael long texts on an almost weekly basis, exclaiming how much it means to him to have a guy friend to talk about things with. However, Paul's texts are long, and my husband's attention span is short. I'd never tell Paul this, but Michael rarely reads to the end of his texts.

"Come on, Michael," I say. "I want to get to know her. I'm curious about a woman who'd be attracted to a cane dancer."

"A cane dancer? What are you talking about?"

Woops. I realized I'd not yet shared with Michael my little Mac's story in which I'd dubbed Paul a cane dancer. Perhaps I would never share it. How much of my sick humor does Michael need to know anyway? Although, in retrospect, Paul is my favorite when I consider the Jeremy, Brad, and Paul 'Triumvirate of Lonely Men.'

"Considering all the anguish Jeremy and Brad have put us through with their attempts to make connections and have dates, I think it'd be a tremendous relief to meet with Paul and his girlfriend," I said. "Regardless of Paul's issues, he's managed to achieve something Jeremy and Brad are still only dreaming about. He's got a real bona fide girlfriend. I think we need to celebrate that."

"I'll see if I can arrange something," Michael said.

CHAPTER 36

I'm No Longer Listening

At what point does one shut down and say, "That's enough?" Michael and I first entered our involuntary voyeurism of seniors stalking sex in June 2023.

A year later, I looked back and felt sadness about that emotionally-charged summer filled with such high expectations and such low returns. I'm sorry Michael and I found ourselves inserted into the uncomfortable and unwanted roles of observers, confidants, and maybe even co-conspirators. Did we somehow unknowingly encourage or manipulate Jeremy and Brad into seeing us in those roles, or had Jeremy and Brad entangled us because we were vulnerable and needy for connections ourselves?

Looking back, while Jeremy and Brad had seemed so desperate for love, I realize now that Michael and I also exuded desperation, not for love as much as for friendships and deep connections. We were still in recovery, and maybe will be forever, from the trauma and isolation of living through a pandemic on the heels of having walked away from forty-four-year-old relationships and roots in Tampa. We were as adrift as these single men were.

We were all in mourning that summer. Jeremy mourned the loss of his wife, and I mourned the loss of my former life in Tampa. We floundered and struggled to find ways to recover and rebuild our lives. I have no idea if Brad was in mourning for anything—he'd been twice divorced but single for decades—but he certainly seemed to flounder and struggle, just like the rest of us.

While Brad had more luck that summer with women than Jeremy did—he managed to see Maggie four or five times for dates and he went both bicycling and kayaking with my friend Chloe—nothing stuck, to his great chagrin.

Jeremy left Eugene in late July to wind his way across the country, and Brad left a couple of weeks later, also to make his way to the East Coast. Michael and I breathed huge sighs of relief when they left town in their RVs, although I knew I'd miss Brad as a bicycling buddy, and I'd miss Jeremy because he was my deceased friend Norma Jean's grief-stricken husband, and I cared about him.

The bottom line, however, was that I needed my psychic energy to focus on my own life. It had been stressful to see Jeremy's excruciating pain and vulnerability, and even more stressful to feel so helpless to make him feel better.

It had been stressful being in the middle between Jeremy and Brad and my women friends. My loyalties generally swung in the direction of sisterhood, but then I'd find myself listening to what the men reported, which was sometimes inconsistent with what my women friends had reported. How was I ever supposed to sift through these conflicting and emotionally-infused stories and reach a plausible bottom line of truth?

There had also been stress between me and Michael, for we often did not agree on what we saw, what we heard, or what it meant. It bothered me that Michael was so quick to choose sides and arrive at bottom lines. He and I could not talk about many of these situations without getting upset at the other's inability to see what seemed so clear to the other. I certainly couldn't talk about this with either the women or the men involved. To have talked about it with other friends, most of whom now knew both Jeremy and Brad, would have felt like a horrific betrayal of trust. So, Michael and I each independently stewed in our solitary perspectives, neither of us able to talk about it between ourselves or with anyone else.

I found myself wanting to withdraw 100 percent of my emotional energy from even hearing about these bizarre dating escapades despite how interesting they were. They were draining me dry. I longed to lose myself in solitary activities like reading, gardening, and writing.

Even the perspectives from my women friends sometimes left me shaking my head. My friend Libby swears all these old men would not be chasing forty-year-old babes were it not for the magic blue pills that seemed to be available on demand to every man who wanted them. My friend Maggie finds the smell of desperate men nauseating. My friend Chloe is so emotionally detached that she blithely enjoyed bicycling and kayaking with Brad without even realizing he had ulterior motives.

I find myself wishing Jeremy had a bit more loyalty to his deceased spouse. Then I feel awful and guilty that I should be so negative and judgmental. But then, my feelings shift again when I have a conversation with Jeremy that goes something like this:

"I think one of the reasons I want to stay away from women closer to my age is my fear that they'll get sick, and I'll end up having to take care of them until they die."

Jeremy's comment stunned me into silence.

"After those eight months of caring for Norma Jean during her cancer and then having her just give up and go into hospice rather than continuing treatment, I was devastated. I don't think I could go through that again."

Michael and I knew Jeremy had not wanted hospice for Norma Jean, but I hadn't registered how angry her decision had made him.

Although my first response was one of shock and anger that Jeremy would feel that way, I realized within moments that it made sense. There might well be thousands of caregiving spouses who feel angry when their loved one dies.

Another knee-jerk reaction popped up. Cancer killed Norma Jean. She didn't give up. She died six days after going into hospice. I felt like shaking Jeremy until his teeth fell out, which was one of my mother's favorite expressions when she'd become exasperated. I continued my silent furious monologue to Jeremy, ranting that every one of us was going to die and that it was the luck of the draw who does the caregiving and who does the dying. And the bottom-line truth was that neither position was very lucky.

Finally, I wore myself out. Just shut the hell up, I thought. You've never had a spouse die so you cannot possibly know how it feels. My internal monologue shifted to a severe bashing and berating of myself for having climbed on my high horse and thinking I might have answers, which I absolutely, positively did not.

It was inevitable that I'd burn myself out emotionally or at least reach a point where my self-preservation drive would activate itself and lead me to proclaim, "That's enough." I vowed that from that point on, if anyone, male or female, started sharing confidences about his or her love life or asking questions about the availability of any of my friends, I'd politely just shut them right up. I no longer intended to listen.

CHAPTER 37
What Have We Done?

Having vowed to no longer listen to the woes of lovestruck old men and their mating games, I thought of other things I'd be happy to ignore. The exhilaration of full-time RVing seemed so long ago it was as if it never happened. I needed to just let the thought of us taking off in the RV again go, for I knew we couldn't return to that lifestyle. We were too old, and the physical issues were too severe. We'd been in Eugene for over two years, and it was time to take stock. It was also time to stop whining.

We were both restless despite our active social lives and the friends we'd made. Had we become adventure junkies after living on the road? It didn't matter. Our four to eight doctors' appointments each month now dominated our lives. We'd probably never take another trip that lasted longer than two weeks. End of discussion.

I had come to believe I didn't fit into this neighborhood and probably never would. The one thing that had consistently brought me joy while living here was gardening. When the existing coordinator for the park's garden club announced she was selling her house and moving to Seattle, two different long-term residents asked me to be the new leader. Another long-term resident recommended that another person and I share the responsibilities, which was what finally happened despite my protests that I knew very little about gardening in the Pacific Northwest.

I found the first six months or so during which my friend and I shared the responsibilities of organizing and facilitating monthly meetings to be stressful. The meetings always felt a little off-center to me, like something was missing and my friend and I weren't "getting it." Then began some not-so-subtle micromanaging from garden club members who'd been around much longer than either of us. Then the newsletter editor started editing and sometimes significantly altering my dutifully submitted writeups about the garden club for the monthly newsletter. It upset me enough that I talked my cofacilitator into sending the announcements each month from then on. I wanted to tell that editor I'd write another blurb when she started paying me royalty checks. I learned from this situation that under certain circumstances, I could act like a total jerk. Yes, I handled this situation badly, just like several earlier ones.

However, this garden club was a historically contentious, bickering group who'd met monthly for years. Under our new leadership, the club's attendance dropped from the typical eighteen or twenty down to about ten folks each month. My friend and I initially patted ourselves on the back that, for six months or so, our meetings had been consistently friendly and enthusiastic despite the poor attendance. But then, that analysis and summation fell apart with the eruption of discord over the feeding of feral cats.

After a year, I pulled the plug and stepped down from garden club leadership despite some gratifying private conversations with folks who wanted me to stay. A couple of long-term residents stepped up to assume leadership, and the group adopted a new format. It was a great relief, and I'm happy to be back to monthly meetings to talk about gardening. I no longer care whether I'm a friend of anyone's outside of those little garden get-togethers. I love to talk about plants, and I rarely miss those meetings.

🛺

It's been great to get back into bicycling, and I know it's been good for my health and possibly added another year or so to my life. But it's been a lonely pursuit, one that Michael and I used to share. I've been unable to find riding buddies, which is disappointing. I met the one serious Spring Hill cyclist on the bike trail one day and knew that she and I were not destined for friendship or even a quick spin together around the subdivision. She'd have left me in a cloud of dust.

I unfortunately got to know this rather intimidating cyclist while management renovated the community clubhouse. Jill, the office manager, had asked Michael if she could store the treadmill in our garage during the three months the clubhouse would close for remodeling. Jill had been under the mistaken impression that Michael was the only person in the park who used this machine. Before long, several residents were giving Michael and me the evil eye, wondering why the treadmill was in our garage and not theirs. The intimidating cyclist was one of those with a furrowed brow, and she even stormed over to our garage one morning while Michael was doing his workout. She must have felt silly standing there, yelling at Michael, who was contentedly singing offkey at the top of his lungs with his headphones on listening to music with his eyes closed. Michael and I were both relieved when the construction crew finished the clubhouse remodeling and Jill retrieved the treadmill from our garage. I sometimes still run into the Spring Hill rider on the bike trail, and she occasionally even condescends to say hello. Still, I think the treadmill loan from Jill, due to no fault of our own, hurt our social standing in our neighborhood.

February of 2025 brought about two events that will likely alter my future as a cyclist, although I remain torn and undecided. I turned seventy-seven years old, and I've felt myself becoming more cautious. I remember the many folks in Spring Hill who commented when I first bought the bicycle in July 2023 that they'd be afraid of getting on a bike at their age. Back then, I'd sort of gloated, feeling invincible and so proud of myself for still being able to ride. But I haven't forgotten that I took three falls on the bike and that I was damned lucky not to have hurt myself. Every time I get on the bike, I find myself wishing it was smaller and lighter. The bike is too big and heavy for me, and as I get older and weaker, my confidence diminishes.

After five flat tires during the first three months of bicycling ownership, I swore I'd never go riding again without a bike rack on our car so

Michael could rescue me when the next flat occurred. With a five-door car, having the bicycle rack on the car made the rear door a royal pain-in-the-butt when we wanted to use the back storage area of the car.

The second bicycle-altering event of February 2025 was the purchase of a new vehicle. Michael and I agree that we will not put the bicycle rack on our new Nissan. Although the vehicle is an SUV and large enough that my bike would fit with the back seats folded flat, I don't think I'd have the strength anymore to lift the bicycle and put it in the car.

The stars seem to be aligning to persuade me to close this bicycling chapter.

After more than two years I can count on the fingers of one hand the number of friends in Spring Hill I ever text or call. There's not a single person I'm in a consistent get-together-for-coffee-or wine relationship. Nor have we found another couple in this place that likes live music, drinking, and dancing.

We've made friends here in Eugene through our wine club membership and from hanging out at Mac's, where there's live blues music almost every night of the week. The wine bar folks are primarily in their mid-fifties, and it's hard to find common ground when they spend their time preoccupied with adult children in their twenties who are planning weddings, launching new careers, and moving out of state. Plus, these folks still work while Michael and I are retired. If that's not enough, this group is physically much more active than our age and handicaps permit us to be. They camp, hike, kayak, and stay up late at night, all of which we would love to still be able to do but can't.

The Mac's gang is mostly within a few years on both sides of our ages, and there's the common denominator of a love of live music, and for me anyway, dancing. However, they tend to be heavy pot smokers, as are many of the musicians. Although marijuana is legal in Oregon, I don't like the way it makes me feel and therefore don't indulge, except for an occasional gummy to help me sleep. I've never been able to find common interests other than music and dancing with these blues lovers despite recognizing that most of them have had interesting lives. I sometimes wonder if it's the weed, retirement, or physical challenges that's left them devoid of most interests in life other than listening to music and getting high. I do know that in a group of elderly people, there will be a significant percentage who live in chronic pain, and pot is a pain reliever. For Michael, the music and casual conversations are enough. I just wish it was easier to connect with folks who are soaring. I worry that it's yet another flaw in my psyche that I want more meaningful connections.

On my darker days, I began to wonder if settling down in Eugene, Oregon was a colossal mistake. But this was where the transmission fell out of the RV, so maybe this is where we are supposed to be.

At the two-year turning point, I began to realize that maybe the problem was not Eugene, nor our over-55 community, nor the ongoing discomfort of watching folks we care about drowning in their loneliness, nor the onslaught of new medical issues, nor all the pot-smokers, nor the frustration of having not made more progress towards making close friends, nor even my existential fear of a future over which I had no control. The biggest problem, without a doubt, was me.

CHAPTER 38

My Shrinking World

The transmission falling out of the RV had been our silly metaphor for when our bodies became too old and impaired to continue the physical demands of RVing. It happened, and while my living space is now much larger than it was before, my world seems to shrink by the hour.

I ask myself two questions: 1. Is this an inevitable part of getting old, that the number of friends dwindles, that the nights of going out each week become fewer, that one's interest in politics, current events, recreational opportunities, and such wanes to the point that one is happy to stay home and play a board game?

The second question I find myself curious about is this: 2. Am I happier or less happy as my little universe shrinks? I'm beginning to sense that the more I stay home, tend my garden, read books, write, and tackle Sudoku puzzles, the more relaxed and at peace I feel.

The years from 2022 to 2024 were mind-bogglers of change and adjustment. I ranted about my new neighborhood, and I raged about the physical changes that keep popping up in both Michael and me. I tackled gardening in an unfamiliar environment, I started bicycling at an age which probably made it a ridiculously unwise decision, and I spent several months tracking the dating exploits of several single men when I should have shown the good judgment to stay out of other people's affairs. I made what I considered heroic attempts to fit in with the over-55ers in Spring Hill with no success. The time was past due for me to grow up, stop frittering my time away on unimportant placeholders, and accept that I was going to die. It was time to prepare for my last hurrah.

How did I want to spend my last few years? We'd plopped ourselves down in Eugene, Oregon two years earlier where we'd known not a soul and had started the terrifying process of rebuilding our lives. We found ourselves surrounded by people and a culture I didn't understand. We entered buildings and met new people after the social isolation of a two-year pandemic in which I'd truly believed we would die. I grieved the loss of the friends and deep roots we'd had in the Tampa Bay area despite knowing I no longer wanted to live there. And most significantly, I watched as the list of our medical diagnoses grew longer and the list of our physical abilities grew shorter.

I felt like a recovering trauma victim, and I started questioning the resilience I'd always prided myself on having. I began to doubt that I still understood the world and could navigate it successfully.

Michael and I had shared a variety of physical activities during our seven years of RV travel—bicycling, canoeing, kayaking, hiking, and walking. Michael is now able to do only a limited amount of walking and not one of the other former pursuits. Cycling and hiking are the only two of the activities I'd consider doing alone, even if I were physically able to do some of the other activities. I ride my bicycle, but arthritic feet prevent any kind of hiking for more than two or three miles.

Settling down meant that Michael and I had to find replacements for all the recreational activities we lost when health problems arose. Michael latched on to the live music scene in Eugene and believed he'd reached Nirvana. He started playing cribbage a couple of nights each week, and he rediscovered the joy of building model cars, only this time with a shop set up in the garage that cost hundreds of dollars in equipment such as airbrush supplies, a ventilation system, and more clamps and accessories than I could list.

Live music was a mixed bag for me, although I enjoyed it and always went out with Michael to listen and meet up with friends. I hated that it invariably involved drinking, though if I had a bit more self-discipline, I could certainly have both listened and danced to music without imbibing. It's sometimes tough when everybody else is doing it.

The live music scene created another, perhaps even more frustrating concern. I have a moderate hearing loss and find it impossible to talk in crowded places with loud music. When we'd meet our friends in these venues, I often felt left out because I couldn't follow the conversations. I couldn't even blame the hearing problems on my age, since the loss was neurological, inherited from my mother, and not associated with getting old, although my age made me feel a little more comfortable about admitting I couldn't hear worth crap.

I settled in Eugene, eager to connect with the writing community. After all, I'd written three books and wanted to meet other authors. I joined the Willamette Writers (WW), Oregon's statewide writers' organization, which was based in Portland, like almost everything else in this physically large but sparsely populated state. I wanted opportunities to market my books, since the pandemic had brought my in-person strategies to a screeching halt three years earlier.

Despite multiple efforts, I never seemed to connect with the Eugene WW Chapter. I'm sure the local chapter must have members in my age bracket, but if so, they didn't seem to spend their time attending monthly meetings. Attendees were usually young, under forty, and most seemed to write poetry, science fiction, or anguished personal stories. Their work made me feel old and tired. I realized I had come up the old-fashioned way, with teachers and mentors who maintained that only brilliant, accomplished writers could get away with breaking traditional rules. Those tired, old rules had worked okay for me, and I felt somewhat unsettled to realize these young writers had more confidence in their skills than I'd ever had or ever would. The local scene did not appear to be a good fit for me, to my disappointment and dismay.

I managed to hook up with a WW online critique group that met weekly. The group was composed of skilled writers, and I seemed to fit in, which felt good and was what I had been looking for. While I received excellent feedback, the group demand of reading and critiquing others' works every week took a big chunk of my time. After two years, I left the group to focus on finishing up my own manuscript.

After a year in Eugene, I joined a private, nonprofit writing group called Wordcrafters. Willamette Writers and Wordcrafters had a fair amount of overlap in its memberships. I especially enjoyed the Wordcrafters' monthly Open Mics and felt encouraged to see older writers taking part in this activity. This private group also had programs that went into the public school system to promote creative writing, and it sponsored an annual writing contest. I better connected with this group when I started judging contest entries and helping in youth programs.

Somewhere along the way as I checked out various opportunities in Eugene, I'd picked up a couple of friends, both of whom released books through She Writes Press, one in the Fall of 2024 and the other in the Winter of 2025. These were both serious writers, and I trade writing pieces both in-person and via email with them for critiquing.

Eventually, I began to feel like I was indeed a part of the writing community here in Eugene. It helped when the Downtown Public Library added my books on their shelves.

My life settled a bit more, freeing up both time and emotional energy, when I abandoned my dual self-appointed and externally-imposed role of dating consultant. I'm thinking the outcomes for Jeremy, Brad, and Paul would have been at least similar had I not ever become involved. In retrospect, I feel embarrassed and guilty for every snarky and unkind thought that every swirled through my muddled brain. I'm also humbled to have been given an intimate peek into the anguish of coping with the death of a spouse and the internet dating world.

Postscripts are in order for my single friends. I am happy to report that Paul and his girlfriend are now into the second year of what looks like a wonderfully compatible relationship. Paul's girlfriend is a beautiful, bright, and funny woman. I've gotten to know her and am proud to call her a friend. These days, Paul's dancing may or may not include his cane.

I am even happier to report that our friend Jeremy has landed square-
ly on his feet. Through one of his online dating sites, he connected with
a woman about his own age who lives in a Chicago suburb. Although I
haven't met her, the woman's Facebook posts show an attractive, effervescent woman with a close extended family, a love of square dancing and
community involvement, and always with a huge smile on her face in
her photos with Jeremy. They are in their eighth month of a committed
relationship, and Jeremy is hopeful that marriage is in their future. I feel
certain that my deceased friend Norma Jean is smiling down on Jeremy
in approval.

The update with Brad is not as clear. One of Brad's two ex-wives in
Eugene passed away unexpectedly, leaving behind a fifty-something-year-
old drug-addicted son, whom Brad had been trying to rescue and save for
decades. Somehow, in the confusion following the ex-wife's death, Brad
went poof to not only Michael and me, but also to Chloe and Ruby, who
were also mutual friends. I reached out to Brad several times via text and
Facebook, concerned about what might have happened to his son, but I
never heard back from him. Chloe was not as gracious. She reached out
once on Facebook and Unfriended him when he didn't answer. She said
she didn't want to be friends with anyone who'd treat others like that.
Brad has always returned to Eugene in May or June from his winters
on the East Coast. Having found ghosting to be an unsettling way for a
relationship to end, I'll probably reach out to him again in the Spring.

It's not surprising to me at all that my women friends remain contentedly alone. Maggie occasionally asks about Brad and follows Jeremy
on Facebook with no interest in seeing either of them in person. Chloe
joined an online dating service for a short time and reported being
freaked out by the desperate men and how quickly they wanted to move
relationships along. After a few months, she cancelled her online dating
membership and returned to hanging out with girlfriends. Shelley somehow became a pariah in the local music scene and now spends most of
her time in her hometown an hour to the north of Eugene.

In Spring Hill, at least a dozen homes have changed owners in the
past couple of years. Both my friend Polly and the former newsletter
editor have sold their houses and moved elsewhere. My takeaway from

the dizzying departures and arrivals? I just need to be patient. If there are folks who irk and rankle, I need to just sit tight and grit my teeth. Chances are high they'll be gone by next year.

As the two-and-a half-year anniversary of living in Eugene approached, I knew I had more work to do in building my new life. In some ways, I felt content that my world was shrinking, but in other ways, I longed for more. But then, what else is new?

CHAPTER 39
Reinventing Myself

Life in Spring Hill Park changed me. In contrast to earlier feelings of stagnation, I began to see that the stability of a fixed address opened new worlds for anything I might want to do or try in the future. Not only did I now have room for "stuff" in my life again, buy I could also begin projects and hobbies that needed supplies, space, and time.

Plants were not the only passion I'd denied myself during the seven years we RVed. I now wanted to explore my creative side, maybe through art classes. I wanted to improve my writing skills, and I longed to read more books. I was motivated to improve my health. And thinking of my doctor's year-long badgering of me to stop drinking, might I finally give up red wine? For the first time, I saw settling down as an opportunity to reinvent myself. Like a do-over, but maybe this time I could do a better job.

I sensed that as I aged, I was returning to former versions of myself, a returning home of sorts, only this time with more awareness. I had gone to graduate school in social work in the early seventies. Lyndon B. Johnson was in Office, and grassroot street-front social service programs dotted every street corner. We students spent two years of school debating two topics: 1. Civil disobedience—To what extent are we willing to go to jail for what we believe? and 2. How do we bring about the revolution?

Do we work from the inside out or the outside in to make institutions more responsive to the needs of the people? The faculty trained us to be advocates, to speak for the millions of disenfranchised people who were unable to speak for themselves.

I had felt so much intensity in my twenties and thirties I could have spontaneously combusted with outrage at the myriad injustices I saw in society. Now, as I dug deeper to understand my life journey of the past fifty years, I realized I'd outgrown the monovision I'd formerly used to view and interpret the world. As much as I might want to be young and naïve again, I knew it wasn't going to happen. Rather than clearcut, right and wrong answers, my life was now composed of infinite shades of gray. The answers that once seemed so simple and straightforward no longer existed. Does this happen to everyone as they grew older?

As the 2024 election unfolded, I found myself caught up in the local political fervor. I volunteered and spent three long afternoons knocking on doors, canvassing for candidates whose views I respected. Looking back, this was a turning point in getting myself realigned with the person I remembered being in the past and was again meant to be. The political climate in Eugene, which I'd begun to view as my comfy blue bubble, rekindled my passion for causes and issues. I'd turned seventy-seven. People my age were dropping like flies, as life in Spring Hill so clearly revealed. If I wanted to make a difference in the world or even eke out a few more personal achievements for myself, the time was now.

Another breakthrough in my thinking erupted. While I'd thought I'd had a good understanding of the -isms of the world when I was younger, i.e. discriminations based on race, sex, religion, physical and mental health issues, LBGTQ choices, ethnicity, and others, I now realized I'd missed a huge and significant one: ageism. Perhaps it takes a certain age and maturity to recognize the subtle but significant ways younger people sometime discount the opinions of older people. I'd begun noticing in some situations with younger folks I'd feel left out of conversations or that they didn't seem to know how to respond when I said something.

This subtle, near-invisible discrimination against the elderly, combined with the indignities of watching my body betray me in the most cavalier and unforgiving of ways, triggered turmoil. Throw in the uprooting after forty-four-years of life in Tampa, three years of full-time RVing during a pandemic, and then settling in a small town on the West Coast where we knew no one, my turmoil and angst felt both debilitating and inevitable. My gyroscope had been yanked from its familiar waters. But finally, almost three years later, I started rising to the surface.

It took two years of Spring Hill residency for me to understand that I was as guilty of ageism as some of those younger folks I complained about who didn't take me seriously. I judged my neighbors because they were old and physically challenged. I didn't want to admit that I, too, was old and physically challenged. I shudder and cringe at my own blindness.

I now understand that Spring Hill is where I belong. It's a quiet and safe oasis from the frenetic outside world. I belong here as decidedly as Eleanor next door had belonged and as Winifred across the street belongs.

I also realize I'm as crabby and as much of a complainer as other folks around here. I may still feel twenty-seven on the inside, but my spirit is as trapped inside my deteriorating old body as it can be, and nothing is going to ever change that. Not the free Pilates class I just signed up for in the hope that I could regain a bit of my lost muscle strength. Not the Zumba classes I'm taking at the senior center, which leave my poor arthritic joints screaming in pain. Not my weekly Monday morning of volunteering at the Downtown Eugene Public Library. Not my excitement over my new Eugene Garden Club membership. Not even my continued bicycling, where I'm now riding about ten-and-a-half miles each outing when I used to regularly ride twelve or thirteen miles. Sigh. My energy level is dropping, and my endurance is dwindling. I do, however, have the muscle strength and energy to sit at my desk and enjoy my new hobby of Zentangle. One day I'll perhaps even buy a keyboard and start rifling through the two huge boxes of sheet music from my childhood and adolescent years of piano lessons.

I've done many things in my life, a few of which I did well and others in which I failed miserably. Despite how much Michael might dream of returning to the road full time in our still unsold RV that sits on a consignment lot out by the airport here in Eugene, I think we both know in our hearts that we'll never do that again. What I will do, however, is continue to write and garden, both of which reflect my strong belief in the future.

I don't fully understand how, why, or when my attitude changed from negative to positive toward my over-55 community. Nor do I know when or what caused the transformation of my reactions to the dating antics of seniors from chagrin to compassion. My outrage at the horrific indignities that my now seventy-seven-year-old body is suffering has mellowed. I seem to now respond with a simple blasé 'so-what' sort of shrug. I've reached a point of acceptance, and it is a relief.

I no longer fixate on the fear of either becoming or needing a full-time caregiver down the road. I have confidence I'll manage regardless of how things shake out, and I'm reassured that while the challenges ahead might be new to me, they are well-known and familiar to folks in my age bracket. It is comforting to find myself nestled in this enclave of old people.

My neighbor Matt across the street is eighty-five. He spends about twelve hours a day gardening, mostly in his backyard. He grows blueberries and raspberries, asparagus and artichokes. How cool. He completed Master Gardener training several years for his own edification, with no intention of becoming certified and giving back to the community. His stated goal for the future is to live to 109 years of age, which he proclaims loudly to anyone who'll listen. Matt believes life in Spring Hill will help him achieve this goal. I don't know Matt that well, but I'd surely like to know how he came up with the number 109. One day soon, when he's working in his front yard, I'm going to walk over and ask him.

I think of Winifred across the street, who recently celebrated her ninety-sixth birthday. She has inspired me and given me hope that I might live long enough to hear songbirds in my little crabapple tree and pick an apple from one of its branches. Maybe I'll even pass away while sitting in a chair in the shade of that tree while reading a book and sipping iced tea. Or perhaps a glass of red wine, which would be even better.

My greatest inspiration these days is from Madeline, our oldest Spring Hill resident whom I don't even know except to say hello at the monthly Saturday morning coffee hours. She is now ninety-nine years old, lives independently, and continues to drive herself around town.

A neighbor recently shared a Madeline story that brought tears of admiration to my eyes. Every Friday afternoon, Madeline drives to a nearby wine bar where she meets her 100-year-old friend. The two women each enjoy a glass of wine as they visit, and then they get into their respective cars and drive themselves home. Maybe I won't have to give up my daily nectar from the goddess after all.

Meanwhile, I find the prospect of a shrinking world comforting rather than distressing. It's fun to nest again, and the inside of my house is beginning to feel like a greenhouse with all the houseplants. My goal is to have at least a dozen that reach the ceiling. (Michael is watching the plant proliferation with concern, hoping there'll remain enough room in the house for him in this rapidly growing jungle.) I read, I write, I garden, and sometimes I go out to meet friends for lunch or at night for a couple of drinks while listening to live music. And when I'm out listening to those local bands, I dance, knowing I'd better do it while I still can.

I'm relieved to have made peace with my mortality. Life in my bubble is good, and I trust that it will remain so even as my world continues to shrink. While the transmission may have fallen out of the RV, the one inside me continues to work just fine.

About the Author

Gerri Almand is the author of three multiply awarded, humorous nonfiction books about RV travel: *The Reluctant RV Wife*, *Home Is Where the RV Is*, and *Running from Covid in our RV Cocoon*. In addition, She has been published in multiple magazines and journals.

Gerri's latest nonfiction humorous book, *Over-55 Conniptions*, begins a new chapter in her life. When health problems brought their RVing days to an end, she and her husband moved into an over-55 community, thus triggering the unmistaken realization that she was now an elderly woman with a time-limited future. In this newest release, Gerri chronicles her struggle to acquiesce to the inevitability of growing old, doing so with sharp humor, poignant insights, and caring compassion.

Prior to writing, Gerri enjoyed a forty-year career as a social worker, working with children and families in a variety of settings. Little did she realize during decades of writing reports that she'd write creative nonfiction books after she retired.

Gerri now makes her home with her husband in Eugene, Oregon, happily nestled in her over-55 neighborhood where she has adjusted and most decidedly belongs. Her hobbies include gardening, listening to live music, and sipping pinot noir in one of the local wineries. Her goal is to expand her large collection of indoor plants until her home resembles a tropical rain forest.